ONE
THOUSAND
BEARDS

ONE THOUSAND BEARDS

A Cultural History of Facial Hair

Allan
Peterkin

ARSENAL PULP PRESS
VANCOUVER

ARSENAL PULP PRESS
103-1014 Homer Street
Vancouver, B.C.
Canada V6B 2W9
arsenalpulp.com

The publisher gratefully acknowledges the support of the Canada Council for the Arts and the British Columbia Arts Council for its publishing program and the Government of Canada through the Book Publishing Industry Development Program for its publishing activities.

Text design by Lisa Eng-Lodge
Production Assistant: Felicia Lo
Chapter title page illustrations: russty-b
Printed and bound in Canada

Efforts have been made to locate copyright holders of source material wherever possible. The publisher welcomes hearing from any copyright holders of material used in this book who have not been contacted.

CANADIAN CATALOGUING IN PUBLICATION DATA:
Peterkin, Allan D.
  One thousand beards

  Includes bibliographical references.
  ISBN 1-55152-107-5

1. Beards. I. Title.
GT2320.P47 2001   391.5   C2001-911288-2

TABLE OF CONTENTS

9   Introduction

15   CHAPTER 1   The Antique Beard: A History of the Beard

41   CHAPTER 2   Beards of Fame and Infamy

59   CHAPTER 3   The Anti-Beard: A History of Shaving

75   CHAPTER 4   The Medical Beard

85   CHAPTER 5   The Religious Beard

97   CHAPTER 6   The Feminine Beard

113   CHAPTER 7   The Unconscious Beard

127   CHAPTER 8   The Gay Beard

141   CHAPTER 9   The Regulated Beard

151   CHAPTER 10   Subsidiary Growth: Alternate Facial Hair Expressions

179   CHAPTER 11   The 20th Century Beard

189   CHAPTER 12   The Postmodern Beard

197   CHAPTER 13   The Personal Beard: Grooming Strategies

219   Resources and Bibliography

ACKNOWLEDGMENTS

For R (alias Petruchio) and his fine soul patch.

Special thanks to furry interviewees, Amanda Miller for limitless help in research and composing style tips, Jennifer Kelly for moral support and manuscript preparation, Helen Godolphin for tracking down all those cool photos, Lisa Eng-Lodge, Felicia Lo, and russty-b for the great design work, and the temporarily clean-shaven folks at Arsenal Pulp.

ALLAN PETERKIN
Toronto, 2002

INTRODUCTION

It was one of those perverse moments of inspiration. Not long ago, I was walking to work at a downtown hospital in Toronto and rather than indulging my own thoughts as usual, for some reason I started paying attention to the faces I passed on the street. I'm not sure at what point it dawned on me, but by the end of my stroll, I noticed that at least one in three men on this busy downtown drag sported some variant of facial hair — stubble, several full beards, goatees, moustaches, soul patches, sideburns, and multiple permutations thereof. When I arrived at work, I decided to continue my survey. Two of the three coffee baristas had goatees, as did the forty-something pharmacist who waved at me. Two of the older men in the elevator had fine white moustaches. Three of my male psychotherapy patients that day also had facial hair.

There was an old man with a beard
Who said: 'It is just as I feared —
Two Owls and a Hen,
Four Larks and a Wren
Have all built their nests in my beard.'

— Edward Lear, "The Book of Nonsense"

I filed the observation away as amusing, but a week later, two events took me deeper into my fascination. On a Saturday night, some friends and I were riding the subway, and a bunch of teenaged girls jumped on, giggling. One of them in pink Capri pants came up to us and asked me, "Do you know what a goatee is?" I replied seriously that it was a partial chin beard. She and her cohorts burst into laughter. "People always rub their chins when we ask. You're the first who didn't!"

The next day I decided to do a web search, one way of checking the current pulse of things cultural. When I typed in beards, moustaches, and facial hair. 2,000 listings popped up (1,580 when I spelled it mustache). I compulsively investigated the first 200, and grew intrigued. In a nutshell, the more reputable pages suggested that almost every man had the capacity to grow facial hair, but historically the decision to actually do so has always come with layers of meaning.

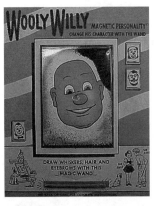

Wooly Willy is a shifty character. His many disguises completely change his appearance.

Wooly Willy game. *Courtesy of Smethport Specialty Co.*

Beards arrive uninvited at puberty, marking a celebrated progression into manhood, but whether they are permitted or even obliged to grow has, until the 20th century, been determined by class, religious beliefs, community precedent, and occupational status. The ancient Egyptians, for instance, viewed hairlessness as an indication of divinity. Only the poor manifested any signs of scruffiness, but that didn't prevent the upper crust from putting on fake beards when the occasion called for it. Periodically in European history, beards were taxed and forcibly removed if one were not upper class or spiritual enough to sport one. Over the span of 5,000 years, chin growths have been purchased, elaborately adorned, dyed, and even deracinated as a form of torture. I learned that the goatees I had just started noticing had actually burst onto the scene in the mid-1950s. The variety of combinations of moustaches, sideburns, soul patches, and beards are virtually endless, as worn by modern men of all classes and ages and social affiliations. Not since Victorian times have male faces been so adorned.

> You would say that each hair of his beard was alive,
>
> And his fingers are busy as bees in a hive.
>
> — William Wordsworth, "The Farmer of Tilsbury Vale"

I had a quick look at other websites and discovered personal pages of men chronicling their own growth history follicle by follicle ("Here's me at three weeks..."). There were endless shaving tips and histories of epilation and sites for collectors of shaving memorabilia. There were celebrity beard pages for actors like Steve McQueen, Sean Connery, and Jonathan Frakes, a.k.a. Ryker on *Star Trek: The Next Generation.* There were societies for sideburn wearers, beard sporters, moustache owners, and even competition sites for the best growths. As always on the web, all roads quickly led to porn ("gruff guys with cum-stained beards" and "hairy bearded chicks"). I took a web-break and started pondering my own associations to facial hair.

My first recollection (always the most significant to a shrink) was a favourite game I had when I was eight years old. It was called "Woolly Willy," a type of wand slate game. Willy had a bulbous nose and a bald head, and he peered out from a plastic casing. He also had iron shavings that could be shaped and fashioned with a magic wand into all kinds of facial hair, turning him into Charlie Chaplin, Abraham Lincoln, or even a girl if you gave him tresses. I spent countless hours, usually during car trips, reinventing him, though I'm certain now that I never even approximated some of the styles I've been studying. But Willy was my first *tabula rasa* of all things furry.

Growing up, my father had only one unshaven friend and colleague, a Brit with enormously bushy sideburns who smoked a Sherlock Holmes-style pipe. He had a tendency to pontificate from behind clouds of smoke and seemed quite the Victorian gentleman. In the early 1960s, my own father, for reasons I have yet to clarify, decided to grow a goatee and to wear a monocle, but probably only for a week (this being rural North Dakota). I don't think my mother allowed any further facial hair experiments except for very modest sideburns in the 1970s.

Naturally, I remembered the beardies of my own development — Santa Claus, the Apostles, Jesus, God the Father, Merlin the Magician, Colonel Sanders, hippies, yippies, and Shaft (Richard Roundtree, not Samuel L. Jackson). My own growth history reveals me to be something of a classic fashion victim. Like all boys, I remember watching, with devoted fascination, my father shave. At one point, I

I mind how once we lay such a transparent summer morning,

How you settled your head athward my hips and gently turn'd over upon me,

And parted the shirt from my bosom-bone, and plunged your tongue to my bare-stript heart,

And reach'd till you felt my beard and reach'd till you held my feet.

— Walt Whitman, "Song of Myself"

The record for weight lifted by a beard is 59 kilograms (it happened in Lithuania in 2001).

World's Longest Beard: According to the *Guinness Book of World Records*, Hans Langseth was buried in Kensett, Iowa in 1927 with a 17-foot, 6-inch-long beard.

There are an estimated 92,370 drinkers with facial hair in the UK (men and women), and they consume on average 180 pints each year. It can be seen that there is UK£ 423,070 worth of beer wasted each year through beard-trapping.

had a plastic razor which I used with his menthol foam. Like the Roman and Greek boys of yore, I was given my first real razor as a gift to mark a rite of passage (certainly up there with my first drink and getting my driver's license): a fine Gillette razor and gel combo, which arrived in my Christmas stocking the year I was fifteen and immensely proud of my lip fuzz. As I look back on it now, the gift from Santa may have been more of a declaration than an invitation. In any case, I started to shave, initially every second day, then daily. It's a ritual I despise to this day, being one of those guys with sensitive skin which sheds, blotches, and bleeds after anything metal is dragged across it.

When I was in my twenties, I grew a moustache, as this was the height of Tom Selleck's fame on *Magnum, P.I.* My moustache was blond and not very tough-looking. And like all college kids, I routinely stopped shaving at exam time, and on weekends, camping trips, or vacations. The year I finished medical school, eight friends and I sailed through the Florida Keys. I have a picture of me with a full pirate's beard, which I wore right through my first year of psychiatry residency. But by the time I reached Montreal, I was no longer a buccaneer. The school I had selected was extremely psychoanalytic, and my beard now paid homage to our Founder. I also suspect that my whiskers allowed me to disguise myself within my new profession until I got better at it. I shaved it off after a particularly gruelling in-patient rotation, thinking it might be better if my former patients didn't recognize me on the street. Abashedly, I have to admit that like my dentist, doctor, and accountant, I grew a goatee in the mid-1990s, until a diplomat friend from El Salvador told me that I looked ridiculous and should shave it off. Which I did. Clearly, I was what fashionistas call a "late adapter" — someone who catches onto a trend as it's already morphing into something else.

The failed chin beard was soon replaced by sideburns, and they appeared for a time on the photo byline of a monthly health column I wrote for the

Toronto Star. Had I consulted a proper hair stylist, he might have told me that they only made my face look longer and rather tired-looking. For the year I wrote this book, I varied between three-day stubble, a soul patch, and an inexplicable urge for a biker Fu Manchu moustache, which I knew I wouldn't be able to carry off at work. Throughout all this, I repeatedly asked myself — why do we do it? Why do we shave like automatons for years, then decide to grow it wild and free? If you actually ask men why they grow a beard or other forms of facial hair, the same answers invariably pop up, several of which I could have provided myself:

- "I hate shaving."
- "I'm balding."
- "I'm beginning a double chin."
- "I want to look more chiselled."
- "I like the way beards look and feel."
- "I was ready for a change."
- "It's more masculine."
- "I want to look older."
- "I just left the military and want to let loose."
- "My family has always worn beards."
- "No one else in my family has ever worn a beard."
- "It highlights my facial structure."
- "It hides my scar/bumps/acne/harelip."
- "I admire Che Guevera/Fidel Castro. (Or any other number of left-wing politicians.)"
- "Women/men like it."
- "It's natural/God-given."
- "I want to look cool/tough."
- "I'm on a holiday."
- "I'm grieving."
- "It's the only thing women can't do."
- "I want to look like my favourite movie/pop star."

Old men and comets have been reverenced for the same reason; their long beards and pretences to foretell events.

— Jonathan Swift

The glory of a face is its beard.

— *The Talmud*

Vir Pelosus ant fortis ant libidinosus. (A hairy man is either strong or libidinous.)

— Latin proverb

All good reasons of course, but they somehow seemed too obvious to me. I wanted to know about some of the other things at work that were popping up in my research. What are the unconscious reasons we wear beards? Why are so many associations dark, diabolical, or subversive? What's the ritualistic symbolism of shaving? What about the gay beard: gender-bending facial hair, bearded ladies, drag kings? If certain beards are archetypal (like Santa or Satan), then what are all of us modern guys saying with our hairy Rorschachs, and why now? Is it rebellion, conformity, or a half-hearted compromise between the two? Do women like beards? Did they ever? What's the post-modern, post-feminist meaning of facial hair? Why are advertisers increasingly using furry models? I was determined to find out, even if it meant asking people on the street and peering at my own face in the mirror as it grew author-fuzz....

❧ *Chapter 1* ❧

THE ANTIQUE BEARD:
A HISTORY OF
THE BEARD

A s I started to ponder beards of antiquity, oddly
enough the first person who came to mind was
my (very much alive) friend Robert. He has
worn a full, classic beard for at least fifteen years. Rob
is an insurance man by day and a member of the
Society for Creative Anachronism (SCA) during most
of his free time.

SCA is a global group of historic re-enactors num-
bering 100,000 men and women worldwide across
thirteen "kingdoms." Periods of interest fall anywhere
between 600 and 1600 AD (perfect, given my own historic query); their staged events feature Vikings,
Medievalists, and various other costumed folk who
battle in armour, fight with swords and shields, feast
at banquets, and partake in music festivals. They also
ponder illuminated texts, study old dialects and man-
nerisms, sketch period dress, and generally have a
great time. Robert estimates that ninety percent of
members have facial hair of some sort, most often full
beards like his own. There is nothing faddish about
these growths — these guys are lifetimers. Which begs
the question: what came first, the hair or the hobby?

In Robert's own case, the seasonal growth predated his historical passion, but may have helped him
find it. He describes his beard as an integral part of
his personality, not just a symbol of his leisure,
adding, "It's like another limb." He frequently makes
oaths by it like his furry forebears, and keeps it
trimmed to a respectful, tidy minimum. Robert can't
conceive of being without his face-warmer. I have no
problem imagining him in battle, swigging ale at a
banquet, or serenading his wife with a mandolin.

Robert wisely reminded me that the history of male
facial hair is, after all, actually a history of disappear-
ances and serendipitous rediscoveries. Prehistoric
man, from the Neanderthal onward (with the exception of a few follicularly challenged aboriginal tribes),
naturally and unceremoniously sprouted beards at
puberty. The history of shaving — a parallel, if anti-
thetical, phenomenon — began well before 2000 BC.

Gradually, in each era, ego reigned supreme. Somebody or other — usually a king or clergyman — instructed others if and how they would be allowed to wear a beard, groom it, or shave it off. Until the propagation of Christianity, which viewed hair as demonic and libidinous, beards were revered as signs of divinity, class, and distinction.

We know the most about the Egyptians, as they fastidiously recorded their habits on papyrus and in tombs. For them, removing body hair was essential as it was seen as base and bestial, but they nonetheless embraced the beard as a status symbol. The beards of kings were usually square-shaped and grew the longest (bigger was better), but were also braided, painted, dusted with gold, oiled, and perfumed. An upward pointed curl on the end was reserved for gods, though pharaohs after death became gods and were thus afforded the same flip. Later on, for special occasions like the flooding of the Nile, both kings and queens enjoyed wearing lavish fake beards made of gold and silver called *postiches*, which were strapped behind the ears like a Halloween mask. Queen Hatshepsut (circa 1480 BC) wore a dazzling plaited variant which left no doubt as to who was boss. Never again would bearded ladies command so much respect. Slaves of course were clean-shaven, so as to be readily identified — a good example of the presence or absence of facial hair being an immediate signifier of stature and status, a much-recurring theme over time.

Like the Egyptians, the Assyrians in the 7th century BC wore both beards and wigs, which were dyed with henna or pitch, and often powdered with gold-dust. The upper crust appear to have spent more time primping, as their beards consisted of tiny curls, arranged in three hanging tiers. (You've seen fine examples in Tintin comics.) Assyrian soldiers, by contrast, were instructed to keep their chins trimmed in due deference.

The Phoenicians and Sumerians were essentially copycats, but the Persians favoured short, pointed

they will ask you whether you will be cut to look terrible to your enemy or amiable to your friend; grim and stern in countenance, or pleasant and demure; for they have diverse kinds of cuts for all these purposes or else they lie. Then when they have done all their feats, it is a world to consider how their mustaches must be preserved or laid out, from one cheek to the other; or turned up like two horns towards the forehead.

— Stubbs, *The Anatomie of Abueses* (1583)

beards, often dyed red with a gold thread woven throughout. (They fought one of the first beard wars when the Tartars tried to get them to wear a religious style they didn't like.) Overall, however, the worthy face during this time was meant to be adorned, and the poor sod who was unable to grow such a status symbol, or who sprouted irregular patches, was seen as ridiculous and beneath pity. As elaborate as facial hair rituals were, it is also interesting to compare them with what was being done with the hair on top of the head. Persians washed their hair infrequently, perhaps believing that spirits resided in one's hair and would be sent down-river. Herodotus, the King of Persia (born 484 BC), washed his locks only on his birthday, a regal prerogative no doubt, but one which must have rendered him smelly and full of nits.

Sumerian king Gilgamesh, c. 300 B.C.

Something of an aside regarding regal hairstyle whims — Mausolus, King of Caria (born 350 BC), of mausoleum fame, ordered his subjects to completely shave their heads and then, in apparent contradiction, made it mandatory to have hair. But he had a more pernicious scheme in mind: he then forced his subjects to buy wigs at inflated prices to replenish his treasury, a stunt he pulled off in other conquered territories.

A quick sampling of other ancient tribes shows that the Tyrians (circa 200 AD), who were fair-haired and blue-eyed, dusted their beards with powder and wove blue beads into them, a look I've spotted in downtown Toronto. The Hittites (400 BC) shaved their beards, moustaches, eyebrows, and the spots above the ears, but wore long, braided side-whiskers, probably the very first sideburns. The much-criticized Philistines of the Old Testament had many flaws, not the least of which was shaving off their beards. Among the Sidonians, beards were like Cadillacs; statesmen and merchants bopped about in long ones befitting their wealth, while soldiers and plebes settled for smaller, functional models.

The Jewish tribes generally conformed to the religious requirement of not shaving hair on the face as per Leviticus 19:27 – "Ye shall not round the corners of your heads neither shall thou mar the corners of thy beard." Some powerful beard stories figure prominently in the Old Testament. In particular, shaving and hair-cutting are considered unforgivable acts of betrayal or humiliation. In perhaps the best-known story, Samson is shorn by Delilah and loses his powers until he brings the house down. A beard is also what ruins Absalom. As you may remember, Absalom was forgiven by David for murdering his half-brother Amnon. Absalom, however, turns on David, but is soon defeated in a forest in Ephraim when somehow his beard gets stuck in a tree. In yet another story, Amassa (in Samuel) is tricked and killed by Joab, when the latter grabs Amassa's beard, pretending to kiss him when instead he is murdering him with a dagger.

Biblical wars are even fought over beards. Take the fight in which Uriah, the Hittite, perished at the hands of the soldiers of Hanum, king of the Ammonites. The war was fought and eventually won by King David. The conflict occurred because the Hebrew ambassadors sent to meet with Hanum had half of their beards shorn by the cruel king. No greater insult could be imagined, as the beard was the man and vice-versa. This unfashionable half-trim meant nothing less than an act of war. (Later on, when we switch testaments, we see that Jesus, who wore the scholarly facial hair of his contemporaries, had his beard tugged and deracinated by his tormentors just before his crucifixion.)

Among the barbarians (a word still laced with bad connotations meaning

Jesus in an engraving by Claude Mellan. *College Art Collections, Stang Print Room, University College London UCL No. 1557.*

Detail of Roman mosaic of Alexander the Great.

His tawny beard was
th'equal grace
Both of his wisdom and
his face;
In cut and dye so like a
tile,
A sudden view it would
beguile:
The upper part whereof
was whey,
the nether orange mixed
with grey.
This hairy meteor did
denounce
The fall of sceptres and
of crowns
With grisly type did rep-
resent
Declining age of gov-
ernment.

— Samuel Butler,
"Hudibras"

"the bearded ones") who eventually led to the demise
of Rome, shaved chins and long moustaches predominated, as exemplified by the Celtic tribes and early
Franks. The Ancient Gauls associated long tresses with
great honour. When Julius Caesar subdued them and
made them shave their heads, there was no greater act
of submission (a form of castration to be studied
more closely in "The Unconscious Beard"). In contrast to the Egyptians, the Greeks were generally hairy
and bearded until the rise of Alexander the Great
(356-323 BC), who initiated a longstanding clean-cut
trend when he instructed his soldiers to remove all
traces of the beard because of its potential to be
grabbed in hand-to-hand combat.

Despite this reasonable (or unreasonable) pre-
sumption, which probably had more to do with the

Great One's vanity than anything else, we now mostly associate the Greeks with their fine beards — from Zeus and his god-cronies to those philosophers who sat under olive trees, stroking their beards and pondering life. Socrates was known as the "bearded master," which subjected him to much ribbing in Aristophanes' Clouds. Hair had tremendous significance for the ancient Greeks, particularly after death. It was cut, torn, or burned by grieving relatives, and the locks of the dead were hung on the door by stricken mourners. By the end of the 6th century BC, the stiff artificial styles of the Egyptians and Assyrians had completely vanished. One exception was Pythagoras of triangle fame, whose hair was assaulted by insects and vermin while on a trip; ever practical, this bane of my mathematical life shaved his head and wore an Egyptian-style wig as a result. But he could get away with it. Generally, Greek slaves were the only shorn baldies, once again to conveniently indicate servitude and to prevent escape. Upper-class Greek boys did not cut their hair until their beards started to grow, at which point it was cut and sacrificed to Apollo. Greek men competed fiendishly over the coif and elegance of their beards — whoever had the most skilled trim-servant was victor.

Aesculapius, the Greek god of healing. *National Library of Medicine, B1093.*

Like my friend Rob, they swore by their beards, but also believed that if you touched a friend's beard while asking for a favour he'd have to oblige your wish. After Alexander's beard-pulling declaration of 323 BC, the clean-shaven face predominated, until Hadrian (117-138 AD) grew a beard to hide facial scars and warts. The beard was back, though once again at the arbitrary whim of a rather vain leader, who naturally assumed that everyone who was anyone would follow suit. Which of course they did.

Early Romans were also a hairy lot, though they issued repeated statements that their beard styles were less "effeminate" than the Greeks. When a slew of Greek-Sicilian barbers arrived in 297 BC, shaving was all the rage until Hadrian's cover-job took hold. For anybody labouring under the assumption that male vanity is a new construct, remember the peacock and read on. Young Romans would let their fuzz-beards grow until they reached the age of majority, at which point they would shave it off and consecrate it to the gods. Emperor Nero did his beard-mitzvah up proud, placing his whiskers in a gold box encrusted with pearls. As in many societies, Romans in mourning would let the beard grow wild and unruly. Reginald Reynolds, in his 1949 book *Beards: Their Social Standing, Religious Involvements, Decorative Possibilities, and Value in Offence and Defence Through the Ages,* delights in recounting the many times when facial hair was either in vogue or hopelessly *passé.* Naturally, slaves had no choice – when beards were chic they were subjugated by shaving, when *déclassé,* they were expected to grow them. The Romans also knew a thing or two about shaving, as they were the first to use warm water, shaving cream (which was oily), and the straight razor. Tarquin, who built the Roman sewer (*Cloaca Maxima*), apparently thought beards unsanitary and is credited with bring-ing the first razor to Rome. The upper classes had their own in-house shave-slaves, but barber shops ready to serve the populace sprouted everywhere. As is still the case, they were the hub for gossip, socializing, and getting the latest gladiator scores. Scipio Africanus is thought to be the first Roman to shave on a daily basis, but he did this obsessively, not once, but three times per day. If we survey the habits of various emperors, we find that Caligula would often wear a faux beard made of gold for special occasions. Hadrian, Antonius Pius, and Marcus Aurelius all sported formidable full beards, while Emperor Julian apparently grew one as a symbolic repudiation of Christianity. Commodus (161-192 AD), known as the

Emperor Julian. *National Library of Medicine, B15844.*

Idle Emperor, had so much time on his hands that he brought back routine shaving. He also proved the adage about devil's work, because as an uproarious joke (and a sadistic one at that), he enjoyed taking over a barber shop, pretending to be a barber, and cutting clients' noses off. From Commodus until the last emperor of the Western Roman Empire — Romulus Augustus — the chiefs were all clean-shaven. Edward, who defeated Romulus and established the kingdom of Italy, started a moustache fad, which as far as I can tell, has never completely faded.

We have very few reliable records on hairstyles from the Middle Ages and must rely on approximations of artists from later eras. We do know that the Gauls, Goths, Franks, and Saxons all favoured long

tease their husband's to vote for you and then you would be President. My father is going to vote for you and if I was a man I would vote for you to but I will try to get every one to vote for you that I can I think that rail fence around your picture makes it look very pretty I have got a little baby sister she is nine weeks old and is just as cunning as can be. When you direct your letter direct to Grace Bedell Westfield Chatauque County New York

I must not write any more answer this letter right off Good bye

Grace Bedell

— unedited letter to Abraham Lincoln from Grace Bedell, age 11

moustaches and shaven chins. Often the head was shaved, too, except for a long tress down the back. Contrary to our stereotypical views of these tribes, this lot paid much attention to their hair-washing and took to setting it frequently with multiple methods of adornment. The Gaul aristocracy, for instance, wove a long moustache, often dyed red, which drooped down both sides of their mouths. Lesser folk wore fuller beards. We believe that the Anglo-Saxons tinted their facial hair blue, green, or orange (though Richard Corson, in his 1965 book *Fashions in Hair*, wisely points out that this information is gleaned from later stained-glass windows which would have been unlikely to incorporate much black or brown). The Middle Ages were a time of long hair and long beards either rounded, pointed, or forked, but only for the nobility. Short, cropped hair was a sign of subservience, so much so that it was duly noted that "to cut the hair of a king's son was to exclude him from succession." The kings of France of the Merovingian dynasty would wear long beards dusted with gold and adorned with jewels resembling a facial Christmas tree. No greater honour could be bestowed on a subject than to give him a single hair from the king's beard or to let him touch the king's growth. Once again, throughout the 6th and 7th centuries, only slaves remained clean-shaven and bald. Norman the Conqueror did not wear a beard before the conquest, but he and his followers assumed them soon after. Charlemagne (circa 768 AD) ordered his courtiers clean-shaven, but he himself wore a long moustache. Later in his dotage, he grew a great white beard which flowed dramatically over his breastplate.

Charlemagne. *Bibliothèque nationale de France.*

The most significant trend of the Middle Ages was when the Christian clergy began to articulate categorical, if repeatedly conflicting, messages about male hair, whether on the face or on top of the head. Throughout the 9th century, Roman priests wore beards while their Greek counterparts were clean-shaven. (A century later, as part of the great schism between the churches, the positions were irrevocably reversed, with Greek Orthodox priests cultivating long beards to this day. I've been to Eastern ceremonies where I feared the priest's longish whiskers would catch fire amidst all those candles.) In 1031, the 7th Canon of Bourges introduced the tonsure of St. Peter (the circular shaven spot on a monk's head) and a clean face for all clergy. Soon after, this Friar Tuck style spread throughout Italy, Spain, and Germany.

For some reason, a semi-circular variant of the tonsure (that of St. John) was picked up by the Scots and Picts, who were never big rule-followers. Edict after edict was issued in the 11th century, and beards were either clipped or shorn completely. In 1073, Pope Gregory forbade clergy to wear beards (though perhaps out of spite or vanity, his own successors, including Damascus II, Leo IX, Victor II, and others, all did so). In 1096, the Archbishop of Rouen, in a fit of pique, threatened excommunication for anyone with a bearded face. Fortunately for all, the very first organization of barbers was taking off, having been established in 1094 in France. It cheerily assisted men in complying with these rather idiotic proclamations, to the sound of "ka-ching, ka-ching." On Christmas Day, 1105, the Bishop of Amiens charitably refused to give holy communion to any bearded man, whatever their excuse for having facial

> He that hath a beard is more than a youth, and he that hath no beard is less than a man.
>
> – William Shakespeare, *Much Ado About Nothing*

hair. In 1160, the Cistercian order of French monks forbade the wearing of beards, in spite of their founding abbot allowing them, provided they were not worn in "vainglory." In 1163, the clergy for once had to swallow an edict themselves. Up until then, priests, as the most learned men of any village, were called upon to perform a variety of medical and surgical procedures. That year, the Council of Tours forbade clergy from performing surgery, ceding that duty to barber-surgeons. As a result, the profession promptly bloomed. Frankly, as I listed all these edicts, I really had to wonder at the Church's repeated interference in matters of the hair. It seems clear that if you had a man by the balls *and* the beard, you had his soul.

The most compelling story I found about antique beards involved Louis VII; the removal of his beard led to an all-out war between France and England. In the mid-1150s, Louis reputedly felt guilty for having burned alive several hundred refugees in a church in Vitry. For spiritual guidance, he consulted Peter Combard, the Bishop of Paris at the time, who told him to shave as penance. Unfortunately, his wife and queen, Eleanor of Aquitaine, was so aghast at his bare face that she had the marriage annulled. Not only that, but she promptly married the much-whiskered Henry II, King of England. When her dowry, including Aquitaine itself, was ceded to England, some 300 years of war ensued. Now we know: the chronic French-English tensions long-ascribed to everything from language to fashion-sense are actually the result of a beard. (I'm surprised no one has ever written a musical or opera about this — how about *La Barbe ou La Reine* with Celine Dion as our fickle queen?) For the married, bearded reader — keep this in mind before doing anything rash with your razor.

Not too surprisingly, by the end of the 12th century, beards fell out of fashion in France. Clergy were ordered to shave twice a month in winter and every ten

This worthy knight was one that swore
He would not cut his beard
Till this ungodly nation was
From kings and bishops cleared;

Which hold vow he firmly kept
And most devoutly wore
A grisly meteor on his face
Till they were both no more.

— Anonymous, "The Cobbler and the Vicar of Bray," circa 1650

days for the rest of the year, with heavy penalties (i.e., lashes, hair-shirts) exacted for non-compliance.

Elsewhere in Europe, beards were often dressed in two points like a barbecue fork and kept under wraps overnight to maintain their shape. Throughout the 13th century, beards, if worn at all, remained short. The French were the overall arbiters of style and fashion, and whatever was hot in France promptly spread all over the continent, or killed the trend that preceded it. The English were not so easily swayed, however. Among those who resisted the trend were Henry III (1216-72) who sported a long, flowing beard, and Edward II (1307-27), ever the gay fop, who chose to wear three ringlets. Poor Edward's narcissism did not protect him as he witnessed the demise of chivalry, feudalism, and the birth of the middle classes before he was murdered with a hot poker up his rectum.

Apparently, for much of the 13th century, so rare was the tufted chin that it was actually dangerous for a bearded person to walk the streets in England. Such a man was obviously a foreigner and would promptly be given the boot.

By the 14th century, beards started to make a comeback amongst the nobility. Once again the clergy responded when, in 1323, the synod of the Church of Orleans forbade beards on priests, hoping for a trickle-down effect. This time, however, even the weary religious couldn't be bothered to obey, so it was decided the rule would apply to "long beards only." There was no stopping a hot facial hair trend in or out of the abbey. Around 1350, in Spain, fake beards became the rage, with men selecting particular colours and styles for special occasions. This fad apparently gave rise to pranks and impersonations of a political bent, so Peter, the King of Aragon, promptly banned them. Meanwhile, back in England, Edward III wore a trademark forked beard that trailed down to his breast; you may remember that Chaucer's merchant in *The Canterbury Tales* wore the same style. Edward also passed eight ridiculous sumptuary laws which restrict-

He lulleth hire, he kisseth hire ful ofte
With the bristles of his berd unsofte,
Like to the skyn of houndfyssh sharpe as brere,
For he was shave al newe in his manere.

– Geoffrey Chaucer,
The Canterbury Tales

ed the wearing of certain colours, furs, and fabrics to pompous regals and their courtiers.

In the 15th century, beards were once again routinely worn by noblemen and elders to signify importance, dignity, and advancing age. They were curled with lead irons, parted at the chin, and plastered into submission. In 1447, during the reign of Henry VI, a decree was issued which forbade the wearing of moustaches and required that the upper lip be shaven at least every two weeks. I could find no historical document to explain Henry's moustache hatred; it may have been seen as the mark of the foreigner or linked to his own inferior growth. Or perhaps he just felt like issuing a decree involving sharp implements that day. In 1461, the Duke of Burgundy was obliged to shave his head for medical reasons, so 500 of his noblemen followed suit, despite a widespread fashion for long hair at the time.

Having reported so many examples of courtiers turning into fashion-lemmings, I was getting tired of narcissistic regals foisting their aesthetic flaws onto their poor, hapless subjects. But then it dawned on me that prior to the 20th century people didn't simply choose hairstyles for the head or face to look particularly stylish or original or attractive, like all us modern guys. Back then, they were worn as a badge of allegiance, whether it suited their unique bone structure or not. The alternative was to be sent to the dungeon, poisoned, banished, or beheaded. (Much, much worse than being mentioned in a "Fashion Don't" column, the worst-case scenario for a millennial celebrity with a failed facial experiment.)

Speaking of tasteless fashion victims, in 1476, the Duke of Lorraine caused quite a stir when he came to the funeral of his vanquished foe, the Duke of Burgundy, wearing a fake, waist-long, gold beard. It created yet another sensational trend, though profoundly tactless in its origins. Although not exactly an example of facial hair, the end of the 15th century brought one final fashion-fright that deserves

Fair of form and proud of mien they are, white and waving both their hair and beard.

— from *La Chanson de Roland*

mention: the Florentine cut, a hairstyle comprised of shoulder-length hair, frizzed over the ears and temples, poodle-style. Very attractive, indeed.

In Europe, the 16th century was largely dominated by just one haircut — the long bob with bangs. It definitely was a time of much precious styling. If a man's natural hair proved to be too short, a wig was worn. Face painting and eyebrow plucking were also a routine part of an upper-class man's toilette.

In 1521, in an incident reminiscent of the Duke of Burgundy's mishap, King Francis I of France had an accident that required head surgery. He had been engaged in a snowball fight when somebody launched a firebrand instead, which landed on the regal's hairdo. (Oops!) His head was shaved for surgery, but when his hair grew in again, he decided to keep it short. Not surprisingly, all of his courtiers followed suit. This obsequiance so impressed Henry VIII of England, that he kept his own hair short and ordered his court to do the same. Full curly beards, Henry-style, finished the look. For some reason I always imagine Henry's beard being full of crumbs and chicken grease, as he did love his food. But he was, in fact, an impeccable dresser.

Back on the papal front, the longest and most notorious period of nepotism, bastardry, and murderous intrigue to plague the Vatican was accompanied by sumptuous beards worn by consecutive Popes from Clement VII (1523) to Clement XI (1700). In this instance, the facial fur was probably an added security measure against the never fully confirmed embarrassment of the 15th century, when a smooth-cheeked woman, Pope Joan, was mistakenly elected to the throne of the Holy See. (Among academics, there remains doubt as to whether this gender flub really ever happened; the closest historical reference

Henry VIII.

points to the illegitimate daughter of Pope Alexander VI, who left her in charge at the Vatican while he travelled on business.) Short of pulling down a curate's pants, his facial hair guaranteed his masculinity and thus protected the Church from female encroachment, and God forbid, the ordination of women. The last period in Roman Catholic history when beards dominated, however, was the 17th century. Never again — including modern times — would whiskers be so omnipresent among western clergy. One of the last great bearded cardinals was Robert Bellarmine, later canonized as Saint Robert, who died in 1621. His long, grey, appropriately named Cathedral-style beard was the subject of an intriguing caricature by some of his enemies — a series of drinking jugs in his likeness were made in Flanders and quickly spread, especially to Scotland. At first they were called Bellarmines, but they evolved into "grey beards." (Before long, any connection with the cardinal vanished, but happily the jugs have survived.)

Pope Innocent X.

Meanwhile, an anti-beard movement was developing back in England. In 1535, the syphilitic Henry VIII had the nerve to impose taxes on those with beards, although he continued to proudly wear one himself. When Sir Thomas More, Henry's Catholic friend, was to be beheaded, he pushed his beard aside on the block and calmly stated: "My beard has not been guilty of treason. It were an injustice to punish it." As late as 1542, members of the English Bar (incredibly called the Lincoln Inn) were not allowed admission with a beard (being defined as "anything over a fortnight's growth"). By 1553, lawyers with beards would have to pay a twelve-pence supplement per meal. France seemed to catch onto the idea of beard discrimination as well. An edict of beards forbade the wearing of long beards in the Hall of Justice. Were they seen as disruptive, untidy, subversive, perhaps too English? The historians fail to tell us. However, back in England, all anti-beard rules were repealed in the 1560s by a growing facial-fur lobby. Yet another reversal for the much beleaguered beard. The 16th century also saw the codpiece inexplicably become a huge fashion hit, confirming there is no telling for taste, even then.

In Germany throughout the 16th century, extremely long beards dominated. Andreas Eberhard Rauber Von Talberg's power-beard was so long, he wore it down to the ground, back up to his waist, and once around (like a belt). Von Talberg was a celebrated knight and preferred to show off his beard while walking rather than letting it dangle passively while atop his horse. An Austrian compatriot, Hans Steininger, was not as lucky in his vainglory. He had such a long beard that he tripped on it on the stairs, broke his neck, and promptly died.

Protestant reformer John Knox.

I was fascinated to note that as beards disappeared amongst the Roman clergy, the emerging Protestants all valued the beard as a visible demonstration against the excesses of the Papacy. (Chances are your prot-preacher still has one to this day and for the same reason!) General fashion styles during this time in Europe included the spade beard (which was either square or pointed), the pique devant, and its very pointed variation called the stiletto. Shorter beards were perfumed, waxed, coloured, and curled. The Marquisotte was cut very close to the jaw line, while the Cathedral beard was long, full, square cut, or rounded, wider at the bottom than at the top. By contrast, the Sugar loaf was grown wider at the top than the bottom. Fork beards were popular as well, and their close cousin, the Swallow Tail, was also worn.

In several European courts, a fantail beard was all the rage. It was three inches long and spread like a fan with much longer waxed whiskers on both sides of the chin; these whiskers were usually kept in a protective bag overnight. Men became devoted to the grooming of their hairy faces. Beards were powdered, waxed, perfumed, dyed, stiffened, starched, and even curled with curling irons. Many of the styles required being kept in wooden presses overnight to maintain their elaborate shapes. (How you kissed your wife, mistress, or page is beyond me; in fact, there is no historical comment on whether women admired such elaborate bristling or not.) All this fussing, of course, lent to the prestige and importance of barbers, royal ones in particular. Thomas Vickery and John Pen were two very famous 16th-century English barbers; they became arbiters of the hirsute hierarchy and naturally encouraged the costly upkeep of the trophy beard.

In the late 1500s, Queen Elizabeth I sent two bearded courtiers as envoys to Moscow. Upon receiving them, Ivan the Terrible apparently delighted in playing with the very long beard of one of them, Lord Kenilworth. Kenilworth nobly bore the strain, no doubt, by thinking of England. Or perhaps he was immensely relieved, as Ivan was not known to be easily amused; he had even killed his own son over a trifle.

The close of the 16th century and beginning of the 17th marked the end of a glorious era in the history of the beard. Initially, the hair grew longer as the beards grew shorter (a recurring inverse fashion trend), although they continued to be waxed, dyed, combed, and protected. A popular style at the time was the Roman T-beard, which was a flat moustache parallel to the upper lip, and a small narrow beard down the chin. Sadly, beards soon disappeared completely for a time, and for the first time since the Egyptians, clean-shaven faces and elaborate wigs dominated society.

. . . no, no, not by the hair on my chinny-chin-chin.

– One of the Three Little Pigs, making an oath on his beard

The moustache outlived the beard somewhat, particularly in Latin countries, but only briefly. They tended to be very thin, oddly shaped, and groomed to curl cheekily upwards.

In 1624, Louis XIII started wearing a wig to cover up his encroaching baldness; only one servant ever saw him *au naturel*. As was becoming the standard, his courtiers followed suit. In jest (and, I would assume, hair-envy), Louis XIII later cut his courtiers' beards off, leaving only a moustache and a small tuft of hair on their chins. Yet another mindless fashion trend was born.

The Vandyke, a goatee variant named after the Flemish painter Anthony Van Dyck, in the employ of King Charles I (1600-1649), grew immensely popular in England and then throughout the rest of Europe. As wigs grew larger and more elaborate through the 17th century, the moustache became smaller and eventually pencil-thin. It finally disappeared when an aging Louis XIV shaved his off in 1680, having, to his utter chagrin, detected grey hairs in it. Apart from pontificating about the Divine Right of Kings at Versailles, Louis favoured minute detail in his clothing, which was usually dripping with gold and jewels. Many of his courtiers went broke trying to imitate him, which led to huge dips in the economy (a small price to pay for basking in the light of one so fabulous). Meanwhile, in Russia, another key moment in beard history was about to take place. Peter the Great, in an attempt to make his empire more "westernized," ordered his nobles and boyars to cut off their beards or face stiff penalties. (I found one anecdote that the proclamation actually came out of an embarrassing moment when a visiting noblewoman remarked on the fluvient from a sneeze dangling from Peter's beard; snotty embarrassment quickly led to stiff taxes.) For noblemen, gentlemen, and merchants of his new capital, St. Petersburg, the beard tax was one hundred rubles per year (approximately forty dollars), paid at the city gates in exchange for a small

"At last the beard is reached. Would he have it shaven, peak cut and sharp and amiable like an inamorato or broad pendant like a spade, to be amourous as a lover or terrible as a warrior and soldado, crates cut low like a juniper bush, or his subercles taken away with a razor, appendices primed or moustaches fostered to turn about his ears, like wine tendrils fierce and curling or cut down to the lip with the Italian lash?"

And then the hair. "Sir, will you have your worship's hair cut after the Italian manner, short and round and then frounced with a curling iron, to make it look like a half moon in a mist? Or will you be Frenchified, with a lovelock down to your shoulders wherein you may weave your mistress' favor? English art is base, and gentlemen scorn it."

– Robert Greene, quip
For An Upstart Courtier
(1592)

copper disk, which represented the beard license. The tax was reduced to sixty rubles for a tradesman or a servant of the nobility, and thirty rubles for residents of the old eastern capital, Moscow. For peasants, it was three pence, not a negligible sum, given the misery of their conditions.

The 18th century seemed to shun beards altogether. They were worn only in isolated cases by the old, mad, or clueless. It was during this century that barbers acquired rather sinister reputations, particularly of being cheats and pimps. One of the popular jokes making the rounds at the time told of a bald man's pricey haircut. The moustache, however, was preserved among the military where it has always maintained a strong hold. In France, for instance, soldiers would wear remarkable crowbar moustaches, and Hungarians were known to favour fine handlebars.

In 1786, French author Jacques Antoine Dulair postulated a return of the beard, but this was seen as a preposterously eccentric idea. The beard was now considered messy and it concealed the "true face," thus protecting criminals and the morally inferior. Arthur Schopenhauer, the sideburned philosopher of pessimism, suggested making a clean shave an absolute law. Later, in Massachusetts in the infant United States, farmer Joseph Palmer was attacked by men with razors on the instigation of the local pastor, who claimed that Palmer's beard was a satanical vice. Palmer fought off his assailants but was jailed for unprovoked assault (he was finally released by the State). The epitaph on his tombstone reads, "Persecuted for wearing a beard." Monsieur Dulair, however, proved to be absolutely right when facial hair returned — in a big way — by the end of the 18th century. Beards on both sides of the pond grew as wigs vanished. Military fashion of the time required the moustache to be long and curled. If a recruit did not have sufficient growth, he was often obliged to paint a 'stache on until a real one grew in its place.

Happily, the 19th century proved to be a complete

heyday for facial hair throughout Europe, with every variation imaginable appearing. It was a boom not unlike today's. Side-whiskers, once only worn by Spanish bullfighters and generals, were re-introduced in 19th-century England. At first they were short, discreet, and never breached the chin line. In 1810, they began to be cut diagonally across the cheeks. Gradually, they became fuller and longer and, by 1830, started appearing well below the chin. Accompanying hairstyles necessitated much curling and waving.

Even outside military ranks, the 'stache was back in a big way. In England, a whole industry of moustache waxes, tonics, and dyes rapidly flourished. By 1840, moustaches and beards were uniformly accepted when worn by prominent politicians, writers, and most cultural figures like Charles Dickens and his U.S. confrere, Longfellow. By 1850, shaving was described as a most peculiar activity, an opinion promoted by returning heavily hirsute English veterans from the Crimean War. Soldiers for most of the 19th century were the celebrated dandies, sex objects, and style setters, and were widely imitated. All pundits were not in agreement, however. John Waters, in the 1850s magazine *Knickerbocker*, reserved particular scorn for the saucer beard (where the face and upper lip are shaved clean, the hair starting at the jawline and joining with side-whiskers). He professed great admiration for the Russian czar for having outlawed beards for Polish and Russian noblemen and soldiers. His lone cry went

Charles Dickens. *J. Gurney & Son, 1867. Library of Congress, LC-USZ61-694.*

unheeded — as there was simply no turning back. Whiskers of all stripes were clearly in for the long run. The Victorian gent argued that beards were natural, God-given, and conferred added health benefits. Shaving them off would surely lead to bronchitis and diseases of the teeth and throat. Furthermore, they were useful in distinguishing men from women, and effectively showed who was boss in the colonies and among the non-converted.

Not surprisingly, American presidents followed the fashion of the day despite its being set abroad. Even Uncle Sam had whiskers added to his clean-shaven face in about 1855. In 1860, apparently at the request of a young girl named Grace Bedell, Abraham Lincoln was convinced that his chances in the upcoming presidential election would be enhanced by his wearing a distinguished beard. He promptly did so and won. (Lincoln's murderer, John Wilkes Booth, sported a less civilized moustache.) Soldiers on both sides of the Civil War (1861-1865) also wore facial hair, in particular, sideburns. In fact, it was Colonel Burnside, something of a flop as a military man, but later a senator, who invented a most distinguished and enduring side-growth that was later named after him.

ABOVE: Abraham Lincoln. *Alexander Gardner, LC-USZ62-13016.*

LEFT: John Wilkes Booth. *Library of Congress, LC-USZ62-25166.*

Mutton chops, long dundrearies, and other 'burn variants, as well as fine moustaches, are clearly visible in photographs of men from the north and the south. From that moment on (though a brief moment it was), with the notable exception of Andrew Jackson, all presidents until Benjamin Harrison wore beards. In comparing presidential growths, Ulysses S. Grant had the hairiest cabinet, Rutherford B. Hayes sported the longest beard, and Chester A. Arthur the bushiest whiskers. Later on, Grover Cleveland, Theodore Roosevelt, and William Taft all wore full, authoritative moustaches. Alas, since Taft, all U.S. presidents have gone the clean-shaven route. In Canada, many Canadian leaders followed the trends laid down by their American and British cohorts, including 19th-century prime minister Alexander Mackenzie.

In 1870, the graduating picture of

ABOVE: Chester Arthur, 1882. *Charles Milton Bell, Library of Congress, LC-USZ62-13021.*

TOP RIGHT: Ulysses Grant. *Perry-Castañeda Library, University of Texas at Austin.*

RIGHT: Canadian Prime Minister Alexander Mackenzie, c. 1873. *National Archives of Canada, C-3892.*

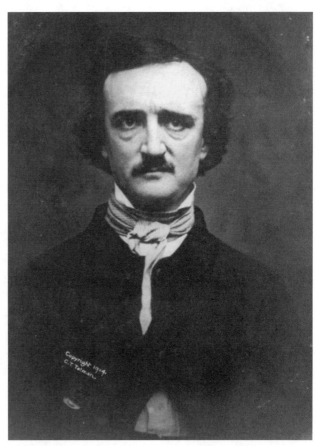

Edgar Allan Poe, 1848. *C.T. Tatman photo of W.S. Hartshorn daguerrotype, 1848. Library of Congress, LC-USZ62-10610*

elite men at Harvard College revealed that they all had facial hair without a single exception. Ivy League styles included the Vandyke, goatee, side-whiskers, and moustaches. (Also of note: it was about that time that men became interested in personal hygiene regimens, bathing daily and changing their underwear once in a while.) From 1852 to 1871, the trademark moustache and beard of Napoleon III were widely copied; the style, called either the Napoleon or Imperiale, was essentially a variant of the goatee. After the Franco-Prussian War of 1870 and the defeat of Napoleon, the impact of French style lessened considerably world-wide. Anglo-style was starking to take precedence. By the 1890s, another bearded sensation dressed in Saville Row suits was Edward VII who became the fashion plate to be imitated across the whole continent, not just in England (sixty years later, "Teddy Boys" would pay him homage.) Because of Edward's considerable influence, you would be hard-pressed to find a Yank, Victorian gentleman, or European powerbroker who did not wear facial hair of some kind. Later, in England, three eminent and eloquent dissidents – Yeats, Wilde, and Beardsley – decried the middle-class beard and went smooth-shaven as an act of artistic rebellion. Arrogant aesthetes as they were, they had identified a striking new social phenomenon – facial hair was now sprouting across classes and was no longer the exclusive growth prerogative of the rich, noble, or military man. Bearded missionaries flocked to "heathens" in China and elsewhere, and must have shocked their reluctant charges with their hairiness, which would certainly have been seen as a most unfortunate deformity by most Asians and aboriginals.

Canadian retail magnate Timothy Eaton. *Metropolitan Toronto Reference Library, T30587.*

By the end of the 19th century, a slight moustache prejudice had crept in: it was increasingly being seen as a mark of the beast. Still, the 'stache endured somewhat longer than the beard in the early 20th century. The advent of the Gillette blade after 1895 and the emergence of a most persistent hygienic movement no doubt contributed to the temporary demise of the bushiest boom in facial hair history. But much more was to come.

NOTE:

Two classic books at the University of Toronto library were subsequently mentioned in almost every other text on the subject I found. One was called *Beards — Their Social Standing, Religious Involvements, Decorative Possibilities and Value in Offence and Defence Through The Ages* by Reginald Reynolds. The subtitle should offer a clue as to the author's writing style. Reynolds is a rambler who goes on tangents and picks up the thread pages or even chapters later. A good example is a far-fetched link between eating horses and wearing beards, which might have been dispatched with a footnote. He cites Italian, French, Greek, and Latin sources without translation and names obscure historical figures without any explanation. Puns abound. Nonetheless, I am indebted because my delight in the sheer detail (scattered as it is) confirmed my own status as a pogoniate (at the time) pogonologist. The second tome, *Fashions in Hair*, by Richard Corson, published in 1965 and happily reissued in 2001, cuts to the historic chase and provides hundreds of illustrations which let me picture Egyptian kings and Confederate generals as I wrote about them.

❦ *Chapter 2* ❦

BEARDS OF
FAME AND INFAMY

Hight Priest Aaron, brother of Moses (c. 1660). *Saris Museum in Bardejov, Slovakia. Originally from Church of St. Demetrius in Rovne.*

The archetypal meaning we now confer to beards comes from enduring links and associations, both conscious and unconscious, made to specific historical, biblical, mythological, and media figures. For most, facial hair figured prominently in their legend (Zeus), celebrity (Chaplin), wisdom (Aristotle), literary skill (Shakespeare), political ambition (Lincoln), or healing art (Hippocrates).

For others (such as Ambrose Burnside), facial hair distinctions such as sideburns or a moustache may arguably have been their only source of prominence. As you read this list, you'll probably notice that you can conjure up the images of many of these men with surprising precision. In fact, what you know about their lives and achievements may be intrinsically woven into the hair on their faces. In other words, their trademark look has somehow come to symbolize the very essence of their character.

Aaron. Moses' big brother and Hebrew High Priest (see Exodus 28: 1-4).

Abraham. Father of Isaac and patriarch of the Jewish people (see Genesis 11-25).

John Quincy Adams. *Library of Congress, LC-USZ62-48839.*

Adams, John Quincy (1767-1848). 6th U.S. president with long sideburns.

Aristotle (384-322 BC). Pupil of Plato and teacher of Alexander the Great.

Aristophanes (447-381 BC). Athenian playwright, and author of *Frogs, Birds, Wasps, Clouds and Wealth.*

Atlas. One of the Titans who fought against Zeus and was condemned to hold up the heavens.

Blake, William (1757-1827). English engraver and self-taught author of *Songs of Innocence and Songs of Experience*.

Buffalo Bill (William Frederick Cody) (1846-1917). U.S. showman and frontier-fringe-type.

Burnside, Gen. Ambrose (1824-1881). Incompetent chief of Union forces in the Civil War, twice relieved of his command.

Chaplin, Charlie (1889-1977). English-born comedian and film star, beloved as "The Little Tramp" and moustachioed satirist of Hitler in *The Great Dictator*.

Geoffrey Chaucer.

Charlemagne (Charles I) (742-814). King of the Franks and later, Roman Emperor.

Charles II (1630-1685). Moustachioed English King.

Chaucer, Geoffrey (1339-1400). English author of *The Canterbury Tales*.

Cleveland, Grover (1837-1908). U.S. president and one of three who were moustachioed.

Columbus, Christopher (1457-1506). Spanish-hired Italian and New World Explorer.

Confucius (Kung Chiu) (551-479 BC). Great Chinese teacher and philosopher.

Christopher Columbus.
LC-USZ62-96899.

Conklin, Chester (1888-1971). This Keystone Cop wore a fake Walrus-'stache.

Connery, Sean (b. 1930). Scottish-born James Bond known for his quintessential sideburns.

Darwin, Charles (1809-1882). Beagle voyageur and English author of *On the Origin of the Species by Means of Natural Selection*.

Charles Darwin. *National Library of Medicine, B5049.*

de Champlain, Samuel (1568-1638). French founder of Quebec (1608) and leader of New France.

Dickens, Charles ("Boz") (1812-1870). English serial-novelist.

Dionysius (also called Bacchus). God of wine, women, and song in Greek mythology.

Samuel de Champlain. *Library of Congress, LC-USZ62-33292.*

Dali, Salvador (1904-1989). Spanish surrealist painter who once used his moustache as a brush.

Einstein, Albert (1879-1955). Moustachioed frizzy haired genius and relativity theorist.

Evans, Joshua (d. 1798). New Jersey Quaker persecuted for his beard.

Albert Einstein. *Oren Jack Turner, Library of Congress, LC-USZ62-60242.*

Fawkes, Guy (1570-1606). Catholic British soldier and Gunpowder Plot participant.

Fingers, Rollie (b. 1946). 1970s pitcher for the Oakland A's and baseball Hall of Famer.

Fu Manchu. Fictional Chinese character of popular detective story series.

Freud, Sigmund (1856-1939). Austrian father of psychoanalysis.

Guy Fawkes.

Gable, Clark (1901-1960). Suave Hollywood star of *Gone With the Wind* and Oscar winner for *It Happened One Night*.

Galileo (1564-1642). Italian astromer and physicist.

Gauguin, Paul (1848-1903). Moustochioed French post-Impressionist, best known for his depictions of the people of Tahiti.

Gibbons, Billy and Hill, Dusty. Bearded founders of rock band ZZ Top. Their third member, Frank Beard, is only moustachioed.

God (Eternal). Also called Yahweh and most often portrayed as bearded and fatherly.

Galileo. *From portrait by Ramsay in Trinity College, Cambridge. Charles Night, publisher, 19th century. Library of Congress, LC-USZ62-7923.*

Goethe.

Goethe, Johann (1749-1832). German author of *Faust* who died asking for "more light."

Hadrian (76-138 AD). Roman Emperor and facial hair trendsetter.

Hippocrates (460-377 BC). Greek physician and father of the medical beard.

Hugo, Victor Marie (1802-1885). French Romantic novelist whose *Les Miserables* was turned into a block-buster musical, among other adaptations.

Hemingway, Ernest (1899-1961). Virile novelist and Key West habitué.

Hercules. Greek god, He-Man and son of Zeus.

Jesus (4 BC – 29 AD). Bearded Son of God, founder of Christianity.

Joyce, James (1882-1941). Irish author of *Ulysses*.

Paul Gauguin.

ZZ Top.

Hippocrates. *National Library of Medicine, B29734.*

Victor Hugo.

Ernest Hemingway with Fidel Castro.

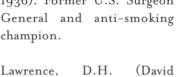

Willie Nelson.
©2000 *Jason Janik.*

King Tut (Tutankhamen). Egyptian King in 14th century BC and wearer of fake beards.

Koop, William Everett (b. 1936). Former U.S. Surgeon General and anti-smoking champion.

James Joyce.

Lawrence, D.H. (David Herbert) (1885-1930). English novelist.

Lincoln, Abraham (1809-1865). 16th U.S. President, encouraged to grow a beard by a young girl who thought he would look more distinguished.

Marx, Groucho (1890-1977). Cigar-smoking, eyebrow-wiggling comic and wearer of moustaches both fake and real.

Matisse, Henri (1869-1954). French painter known for his large figure compositions.

Mohammed (Muhammad). Bearded prophet and founder of Islam.

Henri Matisse. *LC-USZ62-105775.*

Moses. Ten Commandment-recipient and liberator of the Israelis out of Egypt.

McLean, A.J. (b. 1978). Backstreet Boy and snail-trail pioneer.

Nelson, Willie (b. 1933). Outlaw country music star, often matching his beard with long braided hair.

Neptune. Roman god of water and of the sea.

Nostradamus (1503-1506). French astrologer, physician and clairvoyant.

Paul, St. (5 AD-67 AD). Apostle, formerly known as Saul.

Neptune. *Library of Congress, LC-D401-9850.*

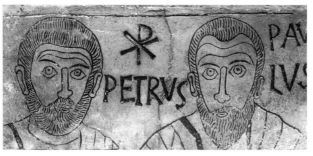

Saints Peter and Paul.

Peter, St. (d. 67 AD). Apostle; regarded by Roman Catholics as the founder of the Church in Rome.

Presley, Elvis (1935-1977). "All Shook Up," but not due to his sideburns.

Nostradamus. *Bibliothèque de la Béjanes.*

Poirot, Hercule. Agatha Christie's fictional, fastidious Belgian detective.

Proust, Marcel (1871-1992). French aesthete and author of *Remembrance of Things Past*.

Raleigh, Sir Walter (1553-1618). English colonizer, writer, and bicycle inspiration.

Reynolds, Burt (b. 1936). Macho actor, one-time *Cosmo* centerfold and owner of classic 70s 'stache.

Roosevelt, Teddy (Theodore) (1858-1919). U.S. president and member of the moustached triumvirate.

Sir Walter Raleigh. *Library of Congress, LC-USZ62-2951, engraving by Simon van de Passe (17C).*

Santa Claus.
LC-USZC4-2275.

Uncle Sam. *James Montgomery
Flagg, LC-USZ62-108257.*

Santa Claus (also St. Nicholas). Jolly fat patron saint of children.

Shakespeare, William (1564-1616). Prolific-playwright and beard-mentioner.

Shaw, George Bernard (1856-1950). Irish-born English playwright who apparently grew his beard when his son asked why he bothered to shave.

Socrates (470-399 BC). Greek philosopher condemned to death for corrupting youth.

Selleck, Tom (b. 1945). Moustachioed eighties star of *Magnum, P.I.*, now alternates between being clean-shaven and not.

Sun Yat-sen (1866-1925). Chinese Kuomingtang states-man, regarded as the father of the modern Chinese state.

Taft, William Howard (1857-1930). Third moustachioed U.S. President.

Uncle Sam. First appeared in the 1800s as the U.S. federal government personified.

Van Gogh, Vincent (1853-1890). Dutch painter of *The Starry Night* grew a beard but cut off his ear.

George Bernard Shaw.
*Perry-Casteñeda Library,
University of Texas at Austin.*

Sun Yat-Sen.

Tennyson, Alfred Lord (1809-1892). English poet, best known for *The Lady of Shalott*.

Thoreau, Henry David (1817-62). Trascendentalist writer best known for his mediative *Walden*, or *Life in the Woods*.

Van Dyck, Sir Anthony (1599-1641). Vandyke-wearer and Flemish portrait painter for Charles I.

Van Gogh, Vincent (1853-90). Iconic post-Impressionist painter, known for his vivid self-portraits as a bearded man.

Wilhelm II of Germany (1859-1941). German Kaiser who triggered a major moustache fad.

Zeus. Top god of Greek mythology.

Alfred Tennyson.

Henry David Thoreau.

Not all facial hair associations are heroic or benign. Very early, as children, we are exposed to images in cartoons, comic books and illustrated novels in which the twirl of a moustache signals villainy, or the stroking of a beard (most often a pointed goatee) signifies diabolical intent. Children's writers and artists continue to use facial hair (alongside pointed features and bulging eyes) as visual shorthand for badness and to great effect. (The historical link between goatees and moustaches and the devil will be explored later on.) Even two-year-olds shudder when any of the furry villains below first enter a frame.

Nous ferons tout ce qui nous plaira! nous laisserons pousser notre barbe!

(We'll do just as we like! We'll grow beards!)

— Gustave Flaubert, *Bouvard et Pecuchet*

Bluto (also Brutus). Popeye's burly, bearded perpetual rival for Olive's affections.

Boris Badenoff. Natasha's Cold War mate and co-conspirator against Bullwinkle.

Dick Dastardly. Relentless schemer from *The Wacky Races.*

Captain Hook. Barrie's archetypal pirate and Peter Pan pest brought to the screen by Disney.

Doc Oc. the octopus-armed nemesis of Spiderman.

The Grinch. Dr. Seuss' green and straggly Christmas-stealer.

Jafar. Aladdin's older rival for power and love.

Snidely Whiplash. Moustache-twirling kidnapper of Dudley Do-Right's Nell.

Yosemite Sam. Bugs Bunny's bumbling, goldrushing nemesis.

Dr. Zin. Jonny Quest's accented, goateed, recurring schemer.

It is an ancient Mariner,
And he stoppeth one of three
'By thy long grey beard and glittering eye,
Now wherefore stopp'st thou me?'

– Samuel Taylor Coleridge, *Rime of the Ancient Mariner*

Osama bin Laden.

Bluebeard (illustration by Gustave Dore).

When it comes to the beards and moustaches of history, it is apparant that the ongoing war between good and evil has often been waged on a man's face. As we'll see, by the 20th century, the unshaven face has taken on sinister undertones of madness, cruelty, satanism and, not surprisingly, "barbarism." Once again, as you peruse this list, you will find it difficult to imagine these villains without their nasty growths. (Nor, it seems, would they have been able to stoop so low without them.)

Alaric (b. 370). Chief of the Visigoths who sacked Rome, which lead to the fall of the Western Roman Empire.

Atilla the Hun (406-453). A ruthless barbarian ruler who was King of the Huns from 434 to 453 and wore an ill-kempt, straggly beard.

Barbarossa (d. 1546). Alias Redbeard, a ruthless Barbary Pirate who became an admiral of the Ottoman fleet.

Blackbeard (Edward Teach) (1680-1718). Famous pirate said to have had whiskers up to his eyes, woven with ribbons.

bin Laden, Osama (b 1955). Contemporary extremist Islamic terrorist implicated in the September 2001 destruction of New York's World Trade Centre.

Bluebeard. Homicidal husband in Charles Perrault's *La Barbe Bleue*. His grisly tale may have been based on the story of boy-killer Gilles de Rais, a 15th-century French marshal, or Comorre the Cursed, a 6th-century Breton chief.

Cardinal de Richelieu (1585-1642). Scheming chief minister to Louis XIII, known as the Red Eminence, and an ongoing aggravation to the Three Musketeers.

Genghis Khan (1162-1227). Mongolian war-lord and famous conqueror. Same fashion-sense as Atilla.

Henry VIII (1491-1547). Broke from the Roman Catholic Church in 1534. Perhaps best-known for killing wives who could not provide him with a male heir (though the fault, as any geneticist will tell you, was his own).

Adolf Hitler. *Library of Congress, LC-USZ62-48839.*

Hitler, Adolf (1889-1945). *Der Fuhrer* who became dictator of Germany in 1933. His "new order" called for the extinction of gays, Jews, Romani (commonly but incorrectly called gypsies), and the mentally or physically handicapped. Is said to have copied Charlie Chaplin's moustache style.

Ho Chi Minh (1890-1969). Goatee-wearer and founder of the Indochina communist party in 1930 whose regime in Vietnam in the 1950s became repressive and totalitarian.

Ho Chi Minh.

Hussein, Saddam (b. 1937). War-mongering president of Iraq since 1979 who launched an invasion of Iran in 1980 and of Kuwait in 1990. According to residents of *South Park*, is the lover of Satan.

Ivan IV (Ivan the Terrible) (1533-1684). Established a full autocracy in Russia and was known for his cruelty, cunning, and love of torture. Killed his own son.

Judas Iscariot. The apostle who betrayed Jesus Christ with a kiss for thirty pieces of silver. His beard was said to be red.

Saddam Hussein.

James, Jesse (1843-1915). Greatest outlaw of the American West.

Leopold II, King of Belgium (1835-1909). Monacled, well-bearded sovereign who developed and exploited the Congo in the 1880s as his own commercial monopoly resulting in thousands of deaths.

Pan. A god of fertility in Greek mythology, a lusty half-man/half-goat with horns, hooves, and the beard of a goat.

Jesse James.
Library of Congress.

Pinochet, Augusto (b. 1915). Well-groomed, pencil-moustached leader of the military junta in Chile that overthrew Allende's government. Now

Pan.

returned to his homeland to stand trial for brutal crimes against the Chilean people.

Rasputin, Grigory (1872-1916). Mad, mesmerizing, and devious confidant of Alexandra, wife of Nicholas II, until his murder in 1916. The Czarina continued to hold seances with him after his death.

Satan. Prince of Evil and God's adversary. Also called Beelzebub (Lord of the Flies), one of the first goatee-wearers (perhaps inspired by Pan, the lascivious goat-boy).

Vlad the Impaler. Legendary 14th-century Walachian Prince thought to be the prototype for Bram Stoker's Dracula.

Werewolf. Legend has it that these creatures are as men by day and wolves by night transformed by the light of the full moon. They may actually suffer from a rare variant of a blood disorder called tralassemia which renders exposure to daylight very painful.

Vlad the Impaler.
Perry-Castañeda Library,
University of Texas at Austin.

Fidel Castro in Washington, 1959. *Warren K. Leffler, LC-U9-2315-6.*

Friedrick Engels.

Che Guevara. *Alberto Korda.*

A final blow to the image of godliness and beneficience bestowed by a beard in western iconography came when it started taking on a red tinge. So enduring is the modern association of beards with lefties, communists, and dictators that millennial politicians are routinely instructed by their advisors to remove all traces of facial hair when running for office.

Castro, Fidel (b. 1926). Now grey-bearded Cuban communist revolutionary and head of state since 1959. Allegedly, the U.S. government plotted to damage his beard in order to shake his confidence and undermine his iconographic image.

Engels, Friedrick (1820-1893). Karl Marx's co-author and editor after his death. His beard was as heavy and as steadfast as his thought.

Guevara, Che (1928-1967). Communist guerilla and hero in Cuba. Killed in Bolivia. His patchy beard is perhaps the most revolutionary and admired of all.

Khomeini, Ayatollah (1900-1989). Muslim fundamentalist who forced the departure of the Shah in 1979 and was acclaimed as the religious leader of Iran's revolution.

Lenin, Vladimir (1870-1924). Founder of the Russian Communist Party and leader of the Bolshevik Revolution in 1917 which overthrew the Czar.

Marx, Karl (1818-1883). Intellectual father of European socialism and author of the *Communist Manifesto* and *Das Kapital* who lived in bearded exile in England.

Selassie, Haile (1892-1975). Emperor of Ethiopia from 1930 to 1974 and cofounder of the Organization of African Unity. Sainted hero of the Rastafarians, who know a thing or two about hairstyles.

Stalin, Joseph (1879-1953). Successor to Lenin who, in 1928, launched massive social reorganization and industrialization, often eliminating enemies in the process.

Trotsky, Leon (1879-1940). Communist theorist and anti-Stalinist who was an instigator of Russia's October Revolution in 1917 and was exiled to Mexico when Stalin succeeded Lenin. Was also Freida Kahlo's lover for a time.

Zapata, Emiliano (1878-1919). Moustachioed Mexican freedom-fighter.

Vladimir Lenin. *Library of Congress, LC-USZ62-101877.*

Karl Marx. *Perry-Casteñeda Library, University of Texas at Austin.*

❦ *Chapter 3* ❦

THE ANTI-BEARD:
A HISTORY OF
SHAVING

As we've already seen, the fortune of facial hair has waxed and waned for five thousand years. If your archbishop said shave, you did so to avoid hell's fire. If your sovereign's beard caught fire, you sympathetically removed your own. Any student of history can appreciate the vagaries of the male ego and the impositions of vanity, but until 150 years ago, removing the beard was no simple task. First you had to find and hire someone you trusted, or wait in endless lines at the barber shop where you might catch something or be robbed. Then you had to endure the pain as your man worked unassisted by such luxuries as proper lighting, hot water, foam, or anything resembling a sharp, unrusty razor blade. He might even top things off by singeing your whiskers using a candle. For centuries, it was inconceivable that you might try any of these shaving techniques at home on your own face. This was an act of necessity, a painful price for belonging to a particular group or class, not an act of lavish self-pampering as we interpret the ritual today.

Having said that, despite everything modern domestic technology has to offer, I must confess that I still hate shaving. In fact, many of my personal forays into facial hair were prompted by loathing of the blade and sheer indolence. I'd classify such growth as "the ambivalent beard." Frankly, short of a few fetishists, I don't know anyone, male or female, who enjoys scraping sharp metal over skin. Yet we spend billions for shaving implements (I am anxiously waiting for the quintuple-blade razor head) and perform the ritual daily.

Advertisement featuring a monkey barber. *National Library of Medicine, A21822.*

And shavers have their share of detractors: as we'll see in Chapter 7, psychoanalysts tell us that shaving is an act of auto-castration to quell Oedipal desires. The Beard Liberation Front of London, a hirsute human rights group, informs us shavers that we are suffering from internalized beardophobia: we'd rather mutilate ourselves than experience the discrimination linked to all the negative stereotypes about facial hair so prevalent in modern society. Many men shave because their partners prefer it, especially when engaging in intimacy, as bristles abrade facial and genital skin. (Women are, at best, split 50-50 in their appreciation of beards, with women over forty generally preferring "a clean-shaven man," while twenty-somethings are more likely to describe "facial fungus" as hot-looking.) Shaving may also be like circumcision — if your dad was "cut," you are more likely to follow suit.

Depiction of Sweeney Todd, "the demon barber of Fleet Street." *Poster design: Andrew Lewis Design © 2001.*

Whatever the reason, shaving is a huge multinational industry that, through clever and powerful marketing, continually seduces us to remove, dye, and precision-trim what would otherwise sprout naturally. As a razorphobe, I simply had to find out who came up with this bright idea in the first place.

Any history of beards naturally begs a parallel history of shaving. The god Mercury was said to have invented the razor, but credit for hair removal actually goes to the much less glamorous. We may think of Stone-Agers as universally fuzzy, but by 100,000 BC,

A 15-year-old boy will trim 30 feet of beard by the age of 80.

Ninety percent of men shave once a day.

Shaving uses up 5 months of a man's life if he starts at age 14.

A man will shave approximately 20,000 times over a lifetime.

60% of men use disposable razors, 20% use electric.

Razors and blades are a $1.1 billion industry.

A man of 80 has likely spent 2,965 hours of his life shaving.

The razor is the most commonly used item by North American males.

man was engaging in activities that some modern primitives still enjoy — filing teeth, tattooing the body, and using seashells to pluck out hair. All this is enthusiastically documented in detail in early cave paintings.

By 30,000 BC, the first disposable razors made of sharp flint appeared; they must have been wretchedly painful. These razors became particularly popular with hunters and gatherers (though what could motivate someone to shave in the bush is something of a mystery to me). Anthropologists now tend to believe that a bearded face lends a man a dominant ferocity, with ape-like "jaw jut" a sign of aggression. The reasons why some prehistoric men removed their facial hair, given the inconvenience and agony, is open to speculation. Perhaps the shorn were required to demonstrate submissiveness to their leader, or maybe Wilma and Betty simply preferred a smooth puss.

By the Bronze Age, metal innovations led to the creation of permanent copper razors. Iron blades first appeared in 1,000 BC. By 300 BC, Egyptians took the whole shaving trend to heart, as they resolutely believed that head, facial, and body hair were animalistic and uncivilized. Priests shaved off their hair and their entire bodies at least once every three days, grooming techniques that were recorded in hieroglyphics. Wealthy Egyptians kept full-time barbers on staff, but for those Egyptians less rich and in need of a shave, specific street corners bristled (as it were) with barber shops. Razors became more elaborate — gold-plated, engraved, and encrusted with jewels — and were buried (as we discover when we desecrate tombs) with royalty. Any enduring stone images of the hirsute from that time represent peasants, madmen, slaves, or, not surprisingly, what were later called barbarians. However, as evidenced earlier, the idea that beards were symbolic of power was not lost on the Egyptians. Both men and women wore *postiches*, or fancy fake metallic beards, for special occasions, like solar eclipses and the flooding of the Nile. Meanwhile, the

Sumerians were perfecting a tweezer device for more precise plucking.

By 500 BC, Alexander the Great insisted that his troops shave to avoid dangerous beard-grabbing in combat, and because he believed it looked tidier. His logic persisted for almost two centuries. In Rome, the rich retained servants to shave them, while the less wealthy would head to a barber who used an "iron novacila," a shaving instrument which tended to rust and grow blunt, cutting many and killing a few with tetanus. But this didn't deter Roman men from seeing a tonsor because, as has always been the case, the barber shop was the heart of local gossip and news. As well, one's class and status could be read by the hair on your face, including whether you were a slave or master.

In 296 BC, the Greek entrepreneur, Ticinus Maenas, imported professional barbers from Sicily to Rome, which meant that professional shaving became even trendier. As is still the case, young men ritualized their first shave, usually at the age of about twenty-one (late bloomers compared to today); they used iron blades with long handles. Friends and elders were invited to witness the first procedure, bringing elaborate gifts. The shorn tufts were then gathered in gold or silver boxes to be presented to the gods. The formidable Roman general, Scipio Africans Major (236-184 BC), who defeated Hannibal, continued to pitch the virtues of a clean shave by doing it three times a day. One hundred and fifty years later, Julius Caesar had beard hairs plucked out individually with tweezers, considerably more time-consuming, but no doubt safer than entrusting his regal throat to the blade of a corruptible servant. Meanwhile, his soldiers were stuck with rubbing their beards off with pumice.

The Greco-Roman world remained

I must to the barber's, mounsieur, for methinks I am marvellous hairy about the face

– William Shakespeare,
A Midsummer Night's Dream

Julius Caesar. *Perry-Castañeda Library, University of Texas at Austin.*

clean-shaven until Emperor Hadrian (76-138 AD), who grew a beard to hide either a bad case of acne, facial warts, or scars, depending on your source. Young men, of course, followed their leader, so facial hair sprouted defiantly once again for several centuries. Galen wrote extensively on barbering, hair-removal, and cosmetics, gaining him much favour with the power-elite, in time he ministered to them as a renowned physician.

In the Middle Ages in Europe, the grooming industry was booming — use of cosmetics, deodorants, teeth cleaners and such, became immensely popular. It could be argued there were religious reasons for such fastidiousness after the schism in 1054 between the Eastern Church and the Roman Church. Western clergy insisted on a shaven face so that Catholics could be distinguished, not only from their lapsed counterparts, but also from "infidels" like Muslims and Jews.

The act of shaving could sometimes be seriously misinterpreted, and the most famous and fatal example occurred at the Battle of Hastings. In 1066, William of Normandy invaded England and took on Harold, King of Hastings. The English were defeated because the Saxon spies mistook the shaven French for priests and not the enemy that they were. What might be called a "clerical" error led to a most devastating defeat.

In 1096, William, Archbishop of Rouen, prohibited beard-wearing, with several other edicts following in short order. Barbers thrived (see below), and throughout the 12th century, the French were almost entirely beardless. One exception to universal shaving was afforded the Crusaders, who were on the road (so to speak) for months to years, and needed to remain inconspicuous in the Middle East. Pilgrims to the Holy Land were also permitted to be bearded, in imitation of the Apostles. Meanwhile, in the New

Young I'd have him too, and fair,
Yet a man; with crisped hair,
Cast in thousand snares and rings,
For Love's fingers, and his wings;
Chestnut colour, or more slack,
Gold, upon a ground of black,
Venus and Minerva's eyes,
For he must look wanton-wise.
Eyebrown bent, like Cupid's bow,
Front, an ample field of snow;
Even nose and cheek withal,
Smooth as is the billiard-ball;
Chin as woolly as the peach;
And his lip should kissing teach,
Till he cherished too much beard,
and made Love or me afeard....

– Ben Jonson, "Charis"

World, aboriginals, who tended to be less hairy in the first place, deftly plucked hair with clam shells. Later, Aztecs took advantage of their close proximity to volcanoes to forge razors of volcanic obsidian. Of course, in pre-colonial, pre-Christian days, they had their own reasons for doing so.

Shaving continued to be somewhat of a treacherous operation until well into the 17th century when a smooth face under a wigged head was required. In 1680, a type of folding razor first appeared in England. Frenchman Jean Jacques Perret conceptualized the first safety razor around 1770, which had a wooden guard along the blade. He also wrote an early self-help book entitled *La Pogonotomie* (*The Art of Learning to Shave Oneself*). The Perret razor was eventually manufactured and its use became widespread in the late 1700s. The invention of cast steel came along in 1740, very useful for razor-making, and a good example of how industrialization created markets for the home.

The French, ever inventive, also introduced the shaving brush in 1748, often fashioned from stiff badger hair, which made shaving more pleasurable and convenient, as soap could better soften the whiskers. This was a start in the link between shaving and luxurious pampering which we continue to embrace today. Even so, most European men continued to be shaved by professional barbers until about 1900. 18th-century French philosopher Jean Jacques Rousseau, however, lamented the "effeminacy of the shaven face," suggesting that men and women should be "more alike in mind than countenance." Shaving, grooming, fussing, and preening all became *de rigeur* in London in the 1800s, thanks largely to a major fop named Beau Brummell. Mr. Brummell, wealthy thanks to an inheritance, dedicated his life to being a fashionable gent, shaving several times a day, and coiffing his hair in three parts, but he didn't quite succeed; he accrued huge gambling debts and fled to France where he died in an asylum, much less stylish, penniless, and insane. No doubt enduring suspicion

Then Pharoah sent for Joseph, and he was hurriedly brought out of the dungeon. When he had shaved himself and changed his clothes, he came in before Pharaoh. And Pharaoh said to Joseph, I have had a dream, and there is no one who can interpret it. I have heard it said of you that when you hear a dream you can interpret it." Joseph answered Pharaoh, "It is not I: God will give Pharaoh a favorable answer."

— Genesis 41:14-16
Joseph interprets
Pharaoh's dream

A box of Good Humor Blades, early 20th century. *Courtesy of Safety Razors and Shaving Collectibles Web Site.*

of the over-groomed male can be linked to his fate. You could be tidy, even "sharp," but never effete or foppish. Meanwhile, Brummell's contemporary, the brilliant and infinitely more practical scientist, Michael Faraday, found a way to add silver to razor blades, rendering them sharper and less prone to rust. Straight steel or cut-throat razors were manufactured in Sheffield, England; their blades were laboriously forged one by one by skilled metal workers. Self-grooming was becoming a huge market and technology, its ever humble servant.

In the late 1880s, the T-shaped razor was patented in the United States, but this blade still had to be sharpened and replaced. A more striking innovation occurred in 1847, when another Englishman invented a razor with the blade perpendicular to the handle.

A box of Jack Frost single-edge blades. *Courtesy of Darryl DeLozier of Brunswick, Ohio.*

The so-called "hoe razor" was easier to hold and to manoeuver and remains an enduring design. Meanwhile, in the U.S. in 1855, King Camp Gillette was born, worth mentioning here because he would revolutionize shaving some forty years later.

Both events paled for a time, however, in light of a Victorian beard boom, when English veterans returned from the Crimean War. Beards ruled Britannia for all but fops and dandies (or "worse") like Oscar Wilde. Victorian gents in all their macho glory were nonetheless great consumers of scents, soaps, and waxes, produced to keep all furry matters in check. Various English treatises at the time described beard shaving as effeminate, unnatural, irrational, unmanly, and ungodly. Scottish purists in particular condemned Sunday shaving as both despicable and sinful. Christianity had once again changed its tune regarding the importance of beards.

For a time, British trends and innovations in both facial hairstyles and shaving predominated, but by 1880, Americans started to lead the race. That year, the Kampfe brothers patented a safety razor which incorporated a wire guard along one edge of the razor to protect the skin. Fifteen years later, Baltimore salesman King Camp Gillette decided that he was destined to strike it rich by marketing something disposable but absolutely indispensable. In 1895, he dreamt up a disposable razor blade, an idea he acquired from a friend of his who had invented throwaway bottle caps. However, no technology for its manufacture would exist until 1901, when he hooked up with William Nickerson, an MIT engineer (and inventor of

King Camp Gillette, depicted on one of his products.

several wonders, including the push-button for elevators). They improved on the safety razor by producing a double-edge blade cut from a template which could be dropped into the top of a T-shape razor, then used, discarded, and more importantly, replaced over and over. In 1903, they went into production — and a whopping fifty razors were sold. But by 1906, 300,000 razors and 500,000 blades were purchased. A U.K. office soon followed. When World War I began, the U.S. government ordered 3.5 million razors and 36 million blades for its soldiers. By the 1920s, a safety razor designed for women appeared, women having been convinced that underarm hair was

Babies haven't any hair;
Old men's heads are just as bare;
Between the cradle and the grave
Lies a haircut and a shave.

– Samuel Hoffenstein

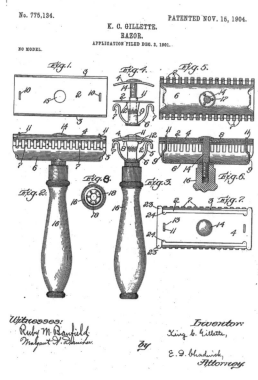

Gillette's original design for a razor. *U.S. Patent & Trade Office.*

nasty and unfeminine.

And what of other shaving staples we take for granted today, like the electric razor or fancy foams? In 1906, W.G. Shockey patented the first wind-up safety razor, which became extremely popular until supplanted twenty years later by the plug-in. In 1925, a brush-less, convenient-to-use shaving cream called Burma Shave came out of Minneapolis, Minnesota, reportedly derived from a native recipe picked up by sailors stationed in Burma. By 1936, it became a top seller and grew in popularity because of an ingenious ad campaign of hundreds of billboards with clever slogans mounted along particularly boring strips of U.S. highway. Sadly, this icon of both shaving and advertising stopped production in 1966, until it was reintroduced by the American Safety Razor Company in 1997.

The next big name in shaving was Jacob Schick, who was single-handedly responsible for the ever present distinction between a "wet" shave (i.e., razor)

Gillette's first safety blade.

and a "dry" shave (i.e., electric), improving significantly on both. He invented and by 1926 marketed a magazine-repeating razor which housed twenty spare blades in its razor handle, advanced with a plunger. The consumer didn't have to touch them and could buy clips of blades as replacements. Of note is the fact that Schick was also a U.S. Lieutenant Colonel, and during one of his stations in some godforsaken cold climate, he injured his ankle and had to crawl out of bed to crack, then melt, ice in order to shave (a story that sounds a bit embellished to me); like all inventors, he told himself that there "had to be a better way." Sure enough, by 1927 he invented the first electric shaver, which used oscillating blades, and two years later he began to sell them. The unit was initially unwieldy because of a cumbersome motor, but by 1931, Schick sold 3,000 at the unthinkable price of twenty-five dollars. But Shockey's wind-up razor continued to give him a run for his money until electric dry shaving caught on, especially for travellers. By the 1930s, most airplanes, ships, and trains had outlets for electric shavers, something we observe to this day. (I confess I have never dared use one, fearing a jolt from the engine or a thrust into the mirror.) Imitators quickly followed. In 1936, Sunbeam introduced the Shave Master. Remington launched the Close-Shaver in 1937, the same year the ingenious Colonel Schick died in Canada. It was clear that as long as men eschewed the beard, technocrats would be at the drawing board whipping up some pricey new twist.

Not long after, Dutchman Frederic Philips marketed the first Philishave electric razor, which had two heads and used a rotary blade. In the late 1940s, a battery-powered shaver appeared, which freed a man from his outlet. Electric razors became part of the masculine cultural landscape, suggesting both affluence and modernity. Many popular films from that era have scenes of prominent actors shaving with dry razors; Jimmy Stewart uses one in *Rear Window*, as does

Hail to the Barber!

Until 200 years ago, no man dared shave himself. The early history of shaving is as much the history of barbers and barbering, as the modern act would never have been perfected without them. Early haircutters were seen as holy men because of an enduring notion that spirits can reside in or be released from hair. Pharaohs had the rites of barbers recorded in tombs. Roman barbers were jacks of all trades — providing advice, wine, women, and song, as well as cutting, shaving, styling, manicures, and massage. They were also the first to use hot water and straight razors. Early Christian clergy enlisted barbers for blood-letting, an enduring cure-all procedure. In 1096, the first European organization of barbers was formed. By 1163, the Council of Tours forbade clergy to draw blood, as the act was believed to defile the body as temple; for the next six centuries, barbers acted as guardians of the leech, performing dental and surgical procedures as well as haircutting. At first, doctors and dentists were relieved not to have to perform such demeaning tasks, but in time they grew rather resentful of their coiffing colleagues. In the mid-1200s, barbers in Paris banded together to form the Brotherhood of St. Cosmos and St. Domain, and founded a prestigious school to train barbers to perform surgery on patients. Its British counterpart, the Worshipful Company of Barbers, was founded in London in 1308, and supervised the practices of the trade in that city. One of its rules was that blood could not be displayed in windows and had to be disposed of discretely in the Thames. Gradually, even more rules were articulated by the profession:

- No handling of razors or talk of cutting the throat.

- First come, first served.

- Boots and spurs, if worn, not to be used for harm.

- Cursing and swearing to be fined seven farthings.

Bay Rum aftershave bottle.

Humphrey Bogart in *Sabrina Fair*. In 1960, Remington introduced the rechargeable shaver and Philips announced a triple header in 1966. By 1969, one-third of men in the U.K. and two-thirds in the U.S. were using electric razors. In 1978, Victor Kiam famously "liked [his] Remington razor so much that [he] bought the company." Until his death in 2001, his television ads proved to be as annoying as they were ubiquitous and effective. By 1981, Philips and its U.S. branch, Norelco, took over Schick's products and trademarks. All the while, electric shaving machines grew more sleek, "masculine," and ultra-modern with elaborate leather (or leatherette) travel cases, suggesting jet-setting *savoir-faire*. But as converts flocked to dry shaving, the wet shave industry would not be outdone. The race for sleek product design and "close, closer, closest" was on. Oregon lumberjacks may still have been shaving with axes in the 1930s, but an entire industry sought to convince men that a wholesome, clean shave could only be achieved by the blade. The Gem Razor Blade Company cleverly coined the phrase "Five O'Clock Shadow" to describe and discourage midday breakthrough stubble. Aftershaves started to appear – in actuality, cosmetic toners and moisturizers, though God forbid they should be called that. Virile-sounding products with associated macho mythologies emerged – Aquavelva in 1935, Old Spice in 1938, English Leather in 1949, and Brut in 1964. Aerosol foam appeared in cans in 1949, replacing shaving soap, mugs, and brushes. As it turned out, even that could be improved on – aerosol gel became the rage by 1990. Not surprisingly, manufacturers of women's cosmetics soon developed expensive "male lines" for the discerning shaver, most often purchased by brand-loyal wives.

Naturally, a market split of the adult population between "wet" and "dry" continued to stimulate fierce competition and industrial innovation. Gillette marketed "long lasting" stainless steel blades in 1960. Though available as early as 1945, cartridge razors reappeared and were heavily marketed in 1965. Plastic disposable razors proliferated through the take-out, throwaway '60s and '70s. (No one worried about landfills back then.) The most popular of these were produced by Frenchman Marcel Bich (of "Flick Your Bic" fame), who introduced his yellow disposables in 1972. A design war proliferated: razors needed to be even more high-tech, scientific, reliable, sharp, and earnest, like the men who used them. If shaving was an unconscious act of castration (see Chapter 7), the man performing it needed a state-of-the-art tool that rendered him macho and restored his sense of self.

In 1971, Gillette marketed a twin-bladed razor called the Trac 2. Six years later, a pivoting head which followed the contours of the face, called ATRA (automatic tracking razor) — an acronym akin to a space age defence program — exploded in popularity. By the 1990s, "comfort strips" were introduced, containing lubricants or polyvinyl perched above blades. The new "sensitive" male of the '90s wasn't afraid to cry and didn't seem to mind being told that he also had sensitive skin. In 1998, Mach-3, a triple-bladed razor, was launched by Gillette after top-secret research allegedly costing almost three quarters of a billion dollars. Interestingly, the advertising budget for all razors seems to have dropped over the last ten years. It is now rare to see advertisements for razor products in magazines or on television or billboards. The market is essentially sewn up, and no doubt companies are throwing their money at some new gizmo, which they will soon convince us is indispensable.

What's next? Quadruple-blade razors? Possibly quintuple? Whatever is in store, shaving is simply too

- Fine of one pint of ale for interrupting barber's discourse.

- Fine of one pine of ale for losing the hat.

- If unable to pay customer shall be sent half-shaved.

After an increasing number of surgical mishaps and misrepresentations of barbers' skills, a 1416 British regulation forbade barbers from treating severely ill clients or those who might be killed or injured unless supervised by a master barber. Until 1461, barbers were the only surgical practitioners in Europe, when their rivalry with medics intensified. In 1540, English Parliament amalgamated the Guild of Surgeons with the Barbers' Company. Alongside haircutting, barbers were restricted to the practices of blood-letting, cauterizing, and tooth-pulling (i.e., no surgery). Nonetheless, they continued to be favoured by royalty and snipped, cut, and bled clients well into the mid-18th century. Henry VIII even allowed them four corpses per year for dissection.

By 1745, the alliance between barbers and surgeons was dissolved by another act of Parliament, at the insistence of the surgeons. By the end of the 18th century, barbers had largely given up surgical and dental procedures, and gradually came to be seen as labourers rather than professionals. The Royal College of Surgeons obtained its own charter in 1800. Over in rural America, out of necessity, they continued to lance boils, pluck teeth, and bleed customers. Barber shops in the United States and Europe were increasingly perceived to be licentious hangouts for gossip, gambling, and even the procurement of prostitutes. Barbers also got rich peddling baldness cures and other snake oils and conjuring up new innovations for the trade. In 1890, the invention of the hydraulic chair made a barber's job infinitely easier. Sadly, by the middle of the 20th century, traditional barbers became increasingly rare,

compelling ever to disappear entirely. It is clear that men have never been consumers of topical products which epilate (a word used by women to distance themselves from the notion of hairiness and shaving), although these substances which remove hair without the need for razors have been perfected over the years. However, in the 1990s, a somewhat more permanent form of hair removal option emerged – laser technology. The trend first caught on with transsexuals, men plagued with excessively hairy areas such as backs, and gay guys wanting smooth legs. Increasingly, however, men of all stripes are using the technology for facial hair, especially if they suffer from heavy growth, sensitive skin, or a tendency to produce ingrown hairs. Here's how it works: melanin, a pigment in skin, absorbs laser energy, and takes it down the hair shaft, where heat actually damages the follicle. If hair does grow back, it is finer and easier to manage. The process is costly – $400 U.S. a session, requiring five sessions for total beard eradication. So far, reaction to the process has been mixed. Few men want to regain a complete baby face, resemble women, or lose the option of having facial hair sometime in the future. Meanwhile, whatever the latest facial hair craze, shaving companies follow them closely; it didn't take them long to unleash a whole new batch of high-tech electric clippers for ultra-precise goatee pruning, sideburn trimming, and soul patch shaping. It is clear that no matter what utensils are available, fashion trends and perceptions of masculine power will continue to dictate whether a man shaves or grows.

Something else became clear to me about shaving as I reviewed its convoluted origins: it's all about ritual. In today's modern world, there are few enduring ceremonies that continue to engage men, no matter what society they live in. Anthropologists tell us that for any true ritual to take hold, the following elements are necessary: an artifact, a script, repetitive re-enactment, and a ritual audience. Men shave with the knowledge they have gained from watching their fathers and possibly their grandfathers, brothers, and uncles over the years. For boys, the act is defined as a masculine pursuit, and an introduction into manhood; although men tend to shave privately in the confines of their bathroom, all shaving-related advertising, with its images of macho-men and the latest phallus-shaped gadgets, confirms this notion publicly. It's no surprise the ancient Greeks and Romans celebrated the ritual of the first shave — the clippings of which were offered to the gods as part of fertility and fecundity rites.

Even now, the youth who shaves for the first time looks in the mirror and he doesn't see peach-fuzz — he sees a man. His repeated use of shaving implements thus becomes part of a complex gender construction in addition to reinforcing prevailing professional, class, and religious associations to "clean-shavenness." In the last 100 years, we have all been successfully convinced that a smooth face is a masculine one. The shaving man uses a man-made tool to reveal his "true face" as he grooms his body and shores up his sense of self for dealing with the outside world. The women in his life are not afforded this enactment (at least not openly or on their faces). The closeness of his shave actually entices the female and becomes part of his competitive edge in the corporate jungle. As rituals go, you don't get much more universal, powerful, or enduring than that. And product designers and advertisers have been aware of it for a very long time indeed.

usurped by "hairstylists," as clients chose perms, tints, dyes, and rather precise hairstyles on their faces and heads.

The barber's pole, however, continues to remind us of the good old days when a man could have his blood let before or after a good shave. The original barber's pole had a brass bowl at the top which housed the leeches to be attached to the client's body for proper bloodletting; many clients grabbed the pole for support during this procedure. The stripes have always symbolized clean (white) and bloodied (red) bandages. The modern pole has a third blue stripe (possibly signifying dusky, venous blood) and a ball instead of a bowl on the top. Today, leeches are making a comeback in wound-healing and grafting, but alas it's the surgeons who control them now.

❧ *Chapter 4* ❧

THE MEDICAL BEARD

Despite the auspicious link between barbering and medical and surgical practices in medieval times, I can't say that in medical school we were ever once told of our historic debt to barbers, certainly not during our surgical rotations. Nor were beards and moustaches and the conditions that befall them ever emphasized, despite the fact that some of the great physicians of the past were whiskered — from Aesclepius and Galen, to Osler, Cushing, and Freud. (I did have one professor of family medicine, a mountain of a man whose bushy salt-and-pepper beard gave him a look of wisdom and experience reminiscent of Moses.) Until the 20th century, beards were a trademark of the medico, probably because of the very visible credibility factor. Two bearded icons who were not doctors, but who looked as if they should be, were the Smith Brothers, whose trustworthy mugs still grace the box of their ever-popular cough drops. William and Andrew inherited the business from their father in 1866. Smith *père* concocted the mixture in the family kitchen in Poughkeepsie and sold bottles of it in the streets. When the boys introduced their trademark box in 1872, it was one of the first factory-filled packages ever developed. Andrew died in 1895, but William carried on the business until his death in 1913, when his son Arthur took over. I have no idea if Arthur sported a beard; I certainly hope he did and that his own descendants carry on a fine tradition.

Smith Brothers Cough Drops package. *Courtesy of F & F Foods.*

It can be argued that beards, as a physical phenomenon, are a distinct dermatological entity, and not surprisingly they have been medicalized throughout history. In the pre-microbial area, their relative merits and hazards were expressed in terms which reflected contemporary mores and attitudes towards masculine appearance and what defined good health. Certain doctors like Adrian Junius in the 16th century proclaimed that wearing a beard protected against a multitude of diseases. The consensus was that the beard was God's will, as evidenced by Christ's beard-wearing, and its medical merits were largely linked to the natural order: beards distinguish men from women. Beards demonstrate robustness of character. Beards protect from the wind, sun, and cold. A good example of these arguments could be found in an early Victorian issue of the *London Methodist Quarterly Review*, which concluded that, "It may surprise not a few when we say that the bronchitic affections, under which ministers of the gospel so frequently labour, are often due to a violation of hygienic law. The fact that the Creator planted a beard on the human male, thus making it a law of his physical being, indicates in a mode not to be misunderstood that the distinctive appendage was bestowed for the purpose of being warm. Moreover, physiologically considered, those who have used or operated by experience for diseases of the throat have in many instances been traced directly to the shaving of the beard. " Those who were without beards, like the "Red Indians" described by Abbé Fangé in 1774, "suffered from poor diet, too much tobacco causing less superfluity in their blood finding its way out of the body in the form of hair."

A few protests or concerns over the wearing of beards emerged in the pre-Victorian era; ideas proliferated that beards might house vermin, catch fire, collect bits of food, or trap the effluent of sneezes. These claims were resoundingly supplanted by other positive arguments suggesting that beards preserved the teeth, strengthened the gums, and protected men from a multitude of respiratory diseases whose precise etiologies had yet to be determined.

In 1864, an unfortunately named medic called Belcher published *The Hygienic Aspect of Pogonotrophy* in Dublin, which detailed the health benefits of facial hair and celebrated its return to favour. In 1880, T.S. Gowing, in his book *Philosophy of Beards*, concluded "the

Beard development is determined by genetics and hormones, therefore one can do little to affect the qualities of one's facial hair or the patterns of its growth.

Beard hair is least dense on the lower cheek, most dense on the upper lip.

Facial hair protrudes at a 35-55 degree angle.

Skin is renewed during shaving and takes 15-20 days to regenerate.

Chain smokers often get unsightly nicotine stains in their fuzz.

Hair grows at a faster rate in the spring and summer than in autumn and winter.

absence of Beard is usually a sign of physical and moral weakness," giving the example of hairless (i.e., degenerate) native tribes, where there "is a conscious want of manly dignity…"

However, as the new science of microbiology emerged, beardliness was coming to be seen to be far from both cleanliness and godliness. Dunkling cites a 1907 experiment carried out by a French scientist who accompanied a bearded man and a clean-shaven man on a walk through the streets of Paris. Both subjects were asked to kiss a beautiful young lady whose lips had been cleansed with antiseptic. A sterile brush was used to collect microbial post-kiss specimens from the lass for the purpose of culturing them on Agar. Whereas the clean-shaven man had a few yeast cells, the bearded fellow was found to have "a swarm of malignant microbes." (I find myself wondering about what kind of young woman would have volunteered for such a distasteful job.)

The advent of World War I introduced a new dimension to the health benefits of a clean-shaven face in that gas masks would not apply firmly to the faces of those with beards, a definite disadvantage when in the vicinity of mustard gas or other toxins. Gillette's new safety razor was also there — in ample supply — to save the day. Beards were grudgingly supported by early dermatology texts which noted that certain skin conditions in men were actually worsened by the act of shaving, such as acne, ingrown hairs, and folliculitis. In such cases, beard growth was suggested as the lesser of two evils.

Over time, reasons why some men were unable to grow facial hair also emerged. For instance, Klinefelter's Syndrome was the name given to the condition in which males are born with an extra X-chromosome. It was determined that boys afflicted with this syndrome maintained smooth faces well into adulthood. Hormonal abnormalities of the testicles, pituitary gland, and hypothalamus — a developing subspecialty of internal medicine called endrocrinol-

When a man or woman has a disease on the head or in the beard, the priest shall examine the disease. If it appears deeper than the skin and the hair in it is yellow and thin, the priest shall pronounce him unclean; it is an itch, a leprous disease of the head or the beard. If the priest examines the itching disease, and it appears no deeper than the skin and there is no black hair in it, the priest shall confine the person with the itching disease for seven days. On the seventh day the priest shall examine the itch: if the itch has not spread, and there is no yellow hair in it, and the itch appears to be no deeper than the skin, he shall shave, but the itch he shall not shave. The priest shall confine the

ogy – described causes which explained other delayed or absent facial hair growth. *Andropecia universalis* was identified as an immune system condition which attacked all the hair follicles on the body, including those of the head, sideburns, eyebrows, face, armpits, and pubes, leaving the patient as completely hairless as a laboratory mouse.

Over 100 years ago, three primary afflictions regarding the beard were identified, and, interestingly, they are still the only three listed in the 2000 edition of *Merck Manual*, a standard medical reference. One is a waxy-scaly affliction called *seborrhoeic dermatitis*. The second is named *tinea barbae*, or ringworm of the beard (barber's itch), a contagious and itchy fungal condition which sometimes affects beard growth if left untreated. The final condition is referred to as *pseudofolliculitis barbae* (PFB), a painful and sometimes disfiguring condition that occurs when stiff hair tips penetrate the skin before exiting the follicle, or grow above the skin and curve backwards into the skin, resulting in inflammation and nodules. Men of African descent are particularly afflicted, with an incidence seventy times higher than Caucasians. Although a special PFB razor is available, topical steroids and antibiotics are sometimes required for managing the condition. Men with a more severe form of PFB, i.e., those with lesions, papules, or scarring, are often encouraged to simply let their beards grow.

One other beard condition that I myself have treated clinically is called *trichotillomania*, in which an individual compulsively plucks out his facial hair, including his eyebrows, leaving bald patches at the site of pulling. Like most psychiatric disorders in the 20th century, *trichotillomania* is thought to be due to a shortage of serotonin in the brain; patients respond favourably to Prozac and its cousin drugs. Behavioral therapy to break the cycle is also helpful. A colleague went so far as to tell me it's pointless nowadays to search for symbolism in these gestures when "It's so easy to treat."

person with the itch for seven days more. On the seventh day the priest shall examine the itch: if the itch has not spread in the skin and it appears to be no deeper than the skin, the priest shall pronounce him clean. He shall wash his clothes and be clean. But if the itch spreads in the skin after he was pronounced clean the priest shall examine him. If the itch has spread to the skin, the priest need not seek for the yellow hair: he is unclean. But if in his eyes the itch is checked, and black hair has grown in it, the itch is healed. He is clean: and the priest shall pronounce him clean.

– Leviticus 13:29-37 (early beard afflictions and the diagnosis of leprosy)

Sadly, a review of the medical literature over the last twenty years reveals little commentary about the beard, either medical or psychological. In the mid-1980s, after the documentation of a condition which later became known as HIV and AIDS, it was revealed that one of the modes of transmission of HIV (as well as other viruses such as hepatitis), could result from the sharing of razors and other implements which drew blood. This suggestion had little influence on a man's decision to grow hair or to shave, but it certainly led to universal precautions regarding non-sharing of razors and other shaving implements. Barber shops also enhanced their sterilizing techniques using autoclaves and ultraviolet light, and many states and provinces went so far as to ban the straight razor outright because of the risks associated with re-use.

The one who is to be cleansed shall wash his clothes, and shave off all his hair, and bathe himself in water, and he shall be clean.

– Leviticus 14:8 (purification of lepers through shaving)

A 1982 article in the *British Medical Journal* by a London psychiatrist named Lacey postulated that St. Uncumber, a devout and hairy young woman who grew hair to forestall marriage to a pagan, no doubt had a form of *anorexia nervosa*, leading to a covering of fine downy hair growth called *lanugo* (see Chapter 6 on The Feminine Beard). According to the good doctor, she was infinitely more neurotic and malnourished than she was saintly.

Another *British Medical Journal* article in 1987 spoke of an Indian gentleman with a very long beard who was encouraged to shave it off prior to surgery. On doing so, it was revealed that the beard concealed a very large goiter, but the story took an even more interesting twist: when the patient examined his beardless self in the mirror, he couldn't handle the shock; he suffered a heart attack and promptly died. For me, this story encapsulates both the medical hazards of wearing a beard and shaving if off precipitously.

A 1988 article in a journal on infectious diseases suggested that bearded men do indeed have a higher incidence of nosocomial or hospital-acquired infections because of the previously postulated notion that the beard traps moisture and bacteria, forming a most effective culture medium. The article did not go so far as to say that shaving of hospital patients should be obligatory, but if you read between the lines, the beard is seen as a risky business.

Surprisingly, a 1994 article in the *Wall Street Journal* carried the headline "China Warns of Beards' Harm." It described an item in China's *Official Disaster Reduction Press* newspaper which quoted an unnamed scientist as saying that facial hair attracts airborne chemical pollution, causing bearded men to breathe air six times dirtier than their clean-shaven counterparts. The same scientist was also quoted as saying that beards led to baldness because they prevented the release of heat through the pores of one's face, leading to an overheating of the scalp; "to compensate, the body drops hair from the head." It sounds scientific, but it's completely false, nor is there one word on how one can actually measure "beard pollution."

In 1995, an article was published in a journal on plastic surgery describing a surgical technique to restore damaged or absent sideburns, in which a flap of hair, still attached to its blood supply, is rotated from the side of the head and sewn into place, to produce natural-looking 'burns. The perils of facelifts on the male face were also discussed, as sideburns were sometimes grotesquely misplaced with Picassoesque results.

In 1996, again in the *British Medical Journal*, Dr. John Curran, an anesthetist, postulated that "beards, a natural state of hairs, signify wisdom." His co-author, Dr. Brian Pollard, contrarily postulated that beards were dirty, "suiting woolly-minded academics disinclined to arise for the morning ablutions." The two authors undertook a controlled study observing sixty-two male professors and eighty-three National Health Service (NHS) consultants in anesthesia. Unbeknownst to the subjects, who were observed from afar at a medical meeting, "facial hair" was defined as the presence of a recognizably maintained beard or moustache;

On the seventh day he shall shave all his hair: of head, beard, eyebrows, he shall shave all his hair. Then he shall wash his clothes, and bathe his body in water, and he shall be clean.

– Leviticus 14:9 (purification of lepers)

The average human male has about 5 million follicles, about 3 times as many as gibbons and gorillas, but still less than the chimpanzee. Average human hair grows at a rate of 0.35 mm per day, or 1 cm per month, 5-6 inches per year.

An average scalp hair "lives" for 3-5 years. An average eyebrow hair only 10 weeks.

Average length and growth rate per day:
Hairs on the head:
70 cm / 0.35 mm
Eyebrows:
2 cm / 0.15 mm
Moustaches (beards or whiskers):
28 cm / 0.4 mm
Armpit hairs:
4 cm / 0.3 mm
Pubic hairs:
6 cm / 0.2 mm

stubble was resolutely ignored. Of the academics, thirty-four percent wore beards or moustaches, whereas only six percent of the NHS consultants did. The study concluded that "academic anesthetists old enough to secrete sufficient androgens to maintain the beard shave less than their colleagues in the NHS." No further conclusions regarding this trend were articulated, although it was noted that various teachers of Islam, Judaism, and Christianity were all wise and bearded in the history of religion. In the end, Dr. Curran established that the association between beards and academic status does not necessarily confirm their mutual undesirability; his co-author ended with a 17th-century proverb: "If the beard were all, the goat might preach." I find it somewhat ironic that anesthetists would engage in such a flip, if amusing, debate, as a number of studies in recent years comment on the difficulty of anesthetizing bearded patients, either in terms of incubating them, applying anesthetic masks tightly enough to make a good seal, or attaching them to respirators. The conclusions of these more serious studies is that beards are a distinct health disadvantage when mechanically-assisted breathing is required. Few surgeons and anesthetists themselves bother with beards nowadays, because they get wet under surgical masks. Now that I think of it, I've never met a bearded surgeon in any of the four cities I've worked, though their 19th-century confreres would all have tied their fuzz in flannel as they entered the OR.

In 1997, Dr. Patricia McNally received media attention for stating that allergy sufferers who washed their moustaches twice a day used fewer allergy medications. Facial hair was described as a pollen-trap, but good hygiene and common sense were the best solution. A report published in 2000 by Dr. Mark D. P. Davis, a Mayo Clinic consultant, showed that Arabic men were at an increased risk for beard dermatitis because of their habit of dyeing their beards as frequently as once a week. The dyes available for this purpose contain PPDA (*para-phenylene diamine*), a compound which commonly produces a rash-like allergic reaction (fortunately, the rash generally disappears after the man discontinues use). It's noted, however, that these days not only Arab men dye their beards; popular new lines of products for this very purpose now exist on every drugstore shelf, so the incidence of this problem will no doubt increase.

For men with weak beards who want to do something about it, transplants are an option. Micrografting is a technique in which small tufts of hair are transplanted from abundant locations (such as the back of the head) to the deficient area on the face. The technique was first described in 1939 by Dr. Okida, a Japanese surgeon, who used it to repair follical defects of the scalp, eyebrow, and upper lip. The technique was largely overlooked in the period following World War II, but now hair transplants of all sorts are extremely common procedures. Their reapplication for purposes of the eyebrow, moustache, and sideburns are soaring to the point where one of the franchised hair transplant clinics, with locations across the U.S. and Canada, suggests that a man can now purchase the "Fu Manchu moustache of his dreams." It should be noted that the technique can be somewhat if not outright uncomfortable, as incisions are made at both the donor receptor sites, with the latter showing evidence of scabbing and redness for several weeks after the procedure. The technique is also not for the impecunious or impatient. It takes between three and five months for hair to take root and grow, two to three treatments may be required, and each session costs approximately $1,000 U.S. or more.

An article on the website *Moustache Summer.com*, entitled "Salvation for the Sparse," summarizes the surgical techniques available for moustache replacement, but also concludes by describing medical trends for the future. Just as lasers can now be used for the eradication of unwanted or ingrown hair, they may be reconfigured to stimulate growth. New hair tonics

Hair does not continue to grow after death. Tissues around it (especially on the face) contract and expose it, giving the dead their five o'clock shadow.

with mechanisms either similar to or different than those of minoxidil (the active ingredient in Rogaine), will soon be available for spot growth or touch-ups. The possibility of cloning hair cells for transplant to desired locations is also noted. All good news for the follicularly challenged, including would-be bearded ladies and those in pursuit of extra-fancy facial hair!

❖ *Chapter 5* ❖

THE RELIGIOUS BEARD

Zeus.

Beardliness has long been associated with godliness. Zeus, Poseidon, Hermes, Pan, Dionysus of Greek mythology, and Thor of the Norse are all fine examples. In his many depictions, God sports a beard, as does Moses (and Charlton Heston) when he receives the Ten Commandments. Jesus and the Apostles all had beards, including Judas, whose beard was said to be a treacherous red. In the 16th century, the Incas welcomed the hairy conquistadors like deities (much to their detriment), because although the native people themselves were hairless, all of their important gods were bearded. By the time they figured out the real gold-digging intentions of the visitors, it was too late.

Throughout history, beards and other forms of facial hair have been important, easily visible signs of belonging (or excommunication) within religious communities. Muslims, Jews, Sikhs, Rastas, and some sects of Christianity all have strong opinions about the beard, its appropriate length, and what it means to cut it. Often it is suggested that those who choose to shave are misguided or worse, infidels.

For modern Western observers, the religious beard often represents fundamentalism, a connotation that has undermined the beard's historical aura of prophetic sanctity and wisdom. (Recurring images of the devil as bearded certainly haven't helped things, either.) It occurs to me that what seems to be simple

Michaelangelo's God from the Sistine Chapel.

"beardism" often disguises more disturbing social attitudes like racism, including anti-Muslim or antisemitic sentiment, xenophobia, and the assumed superiority of a brand of Christianity espoused by the religious right. ("Those people have beards. We remain clean-shaven and on the right track." Perhaps that's what all those 11th-century edicts against facial hair were really about.) Even now

God from a painting by William Blake.

in the aftermath of the devastating New York World Trade Center attack, a new battle between "the sickle and the cross" is being waged, and a resurgence of anti-beard, anti-Islam sentiment may well be directed towards observant Muslims."

MUSLIMS

Mohammed the prophet (570-632 AD), instructed his followers to cut their moustaches and to allow their beards to grow. The beard was defined as hair on the cheeks and jaws, but also included the temples, growth under the lower lip, chin hair, and sideburns. It is believed that Mohammed insisted on this display so as to distinguish Muslims from the long-moustached Magians, who were Persian fire worshippers. Growing a beard and moustache is thus mandatory for all men capable of doing so; it represents two of the ten Muslim qualities of "a good and clean nature." Any attempts to remove facial hair are seen as disobedience to Allah and the Messenger, and are described as

References to facial hair in the Koran include:

Hadith – Bukhari 7:781, Narrated Ibn Umar

Allah's Apostle said, "Cut the moustaches short and leave the beard [as it is]."

Hadith – Muslim, Narrated Abu Hurayrah

The messenger of Allah said: "Trim closely the moustache, and grow a beard, and thus act against the fire-worshippers."

Hadith – Bukhari 9:651, Narrated Abu Sa'id Al-Khudri

The Prophet said, "There will emerge from the East some people who will recite the Qur'an but it will not exceed their throats and who will go out of the religion as an arrow passes through the game, and they will never come back to it

unless the arrow comes
back to the middle of
the bow." The people
asked, "What will their
signs be?" He said,
"Their sign will be the
habit of shaving."

Hadith — Muwatta 51. 7

Yahya related to me
from Malik from Zayd
ibn Aslam that Ata ibn
Yasar told him that the
Messenger of Allah was
in the mosque when a
man came in with
dishevelled hair and
beard. The Messenger
of Allah motioned with
his hand that he should
be sent out to groom his
hair and beard. The
man did so and then
returned. The
Messenger of Allah said,
"Isn't this better than
that one of you should
come with his head
dishevelled, as if he were
a shaytan?"

disfiguring, effeminate, contrary to nature, and an imitation of non-believers. The beard signifies the natural differences between men and women, and its removal is seen as self-mutilation. Shortening may be allowed, if no more than a handful of hair is removed. To swear by the Prophet's beard is still the most significant oath amongst Orthodox Muslims.

There are four schools of thought in Islam regarding the question of shaving. The Hanafis stipulate that it is forbidden for a man to shave a beard or to cut any amount of hair in excess of a handful. The Malikies prohibit shaving if it leads to disfigurement of any sort, but allow lesser cutting. The Shafi'is state that removing the beard is *Haram* (forbidden). The Hanbalis also agree that shaving the beard is absolutely forbidden. Brother Bilal Az-Zuhri, in an Internet article entitled "The Islamic Ruling on Shaving the Beard," cites the following proof for the prohibition of shaving in the Koran: "Allah cursed him. And he said, I will take an important portion of your slaves. Verily I will mislead them and surely I will arouse in them false desires, and certainly I will order them to slit the ears of cattle, and indeed I will order them to change the nature created by Allah. And whoever takes Shaytaan as a Wali instead of Allah, has surely suffered a manifest loss." This quote is accepted as direct evidence that any alteration of Allah's creation without His permission represents disobedience. Further, debates exist as to whether restrictions apply to both the beard's length and width. Scripture suggests that it may even be justifiable to beat a man who has shaved off his moustache.

SIKHS

ikhs, the followers of Gobind Singh (1666-1708), belong to a monotheistic religion where five symbols or emblems signify the Khalsa. These are commonly known as the Five Ks, thought to be articulated by the followers of Singh: Kesa, which signifies the wearing of long hair with an unshorn beard; Kangha, which represents the comb that keeps the hair tidy under the turban; Kacch, the knee-length drawers or bloomers worn by believers; Kara, the steel bracelets worn as a charm against evil on the right arm; and Kirpan, the sabre or dagger worn discreetly. The Five Ks have no actual basis in scripture, but are mentioned by Singh's followers in *Rahatnamai*. It remains the greatest humiliation for a Sikh man to have the hair on his head or on his face cut off or disfigured. Several key legal precedents now exist where Sikhs have challenged workplace interdictions on the beard and won the right to keep them in a multitude of occupational settings on religious grounds (see Chapter 9).

Some time afterward, the king of the Ammonites died, and his son Hanun succeeded him. David said, "I will deal loyally with Hanun son of Nahash, just as his father dealt loyally with me." So David sent envoys to console him concerning his father. When David's envoys came into the land of the Ammonites, the princes of the Ammonites said to their lord Hanun, "Do you really think that David is honoring your father just because he has sent messengers with condolences to you? Has not David sent his envoys to you to search the city, to spy it out, and to overthrow it? So Hanun seized David's envoys, shaved off half the beard of each, cut off their garments in the middle

For Jews, instructions on the wearing of beards can be found in Leviticus (19:26-28): "Ye shall not eat anything with the blood. Neither shall you use enchantment nor observe times. Ye shall not round the corners of your heads. Neither shalt thou mar the corners of thy beard. Ye shall not make any cuttings in your flesh for the dead nor print any marks upon you. I am Yahweh." Much debate exists around the use of the word "mar" (*Schachath*), which is variously translated as ruin, decay, perish, cast-off, corrupt, or destroy. Orthodox Jews and the Hassidim have come to take marring as signifying the use of shaving implements. I discovered that scissors, or electric razors which mimic the action of scissors, are thought to be acceptable in grooming practices. However, absolutely no cutting of the temple hair, or the upper sideburn (*peyos*), is permitted, although trimming is allowed. Elders of the people were called *Zaken* (the long-bearded). I still consider the long Rabinnical beard as the epitome of scholarliness.

It becomes clear that historically, Jews used the beard to distinguish themselves from their enemies, including the Romans, Egyptians, and early Christians. I found it pertinent to modern fads that the above-cited injunction in Leviticus also includes rounding the corner of the head, which means to create baldness. "Printing any marks upon you" signifies the use of tattooing, also forbidden. (I wonder if some of the Jewish rave-kids I've met over the years are aware of this injunction. I'm sure their parents are.)

Leviticus 21:116-18 considers the hair stylings of priests: it suggests that whenever a priest alters his countenance, the image he was created with, he becomes disfigured or blemished. If shorn, the priest would be obliged to wait until his hair had regrown and he had "healed" before once again performing spiritual duties. As is the case with Sikhs, the forced shaving of beards is historically considered a profound insult for Jews. This happened in Samuel 10:4-5, when King David's men had half their beards shaved off. It was also a common phenomenon inflicted on Jewish men in the camps during the Holocaust. (I once met an elderly man with widespread facial scarring; he told me that he had never experienced such pain and humiliation as when handfuls of hair were being yanked from his face by laughing prison guards.) *Yahweh* will not hold a man accountable if he is unable to grow a beard for physical reasons, or loses it through medical illness (or torture). Non-Orthodox or Reform Jews may opt to shave daily, but desist when they sit *Shiva*, a seven-day mourning ritual, as the beard in this case is a visible sign of bereavement.

at their hips, and sent them away. When David was told, he went to meet them, for the men were greatly ashamed. The king said, "Remain at Jericho until your beards have grown, and then return."

– Samuel 10:1-5
(the half shave as humiliation)

CHRISTIANITY

Although the Old Testament abounds with references to the beard and other forms of facial hair, the New Testament is strangely silent, even though Christ wore the beard of His contemporaries. This surprising absence of commentary has allowed theologians to conclude that a Christian man was either obliged to shave, to grow a beard, or to defer the decision altogether: I have seen paintings where Christ is represented as shaven just prior to the crucifixion. This depicts the above mentioned insult of removing a Jewish man's beard as an act of degradation.

As described earlier, the Church went somewhat overboard when it came to beards, reversing their policies again and again, none of which were actually based in scripture. Reynolds tells us that religious

Jesus in a painting by Hieronymous Bosch.

communities became increasingly regulated with respect to the obligations of the novice or senior monk. In Aix-La-Chapellein in 817 AD, for instance,

Saint Augustine. *Perry-Castañeda Library, University of Texas at Austin.*

French monks were instructed to shave every two weeks, but were forbidden from doing so during certain seasons or on particular religious feasts. The later Sempringham rule instructed canons to shave no more than seventeen times per year. The Carthusians shaved their faces six times a year, but the Carthusian rule specified that lay brothers (i.e., non-monks) were forbidden to shave their heads. They were to be charitably distinguished as lesser illiterati or barbati, "the bearded ones." The rule of St. Columbanus gave instruction for any unshaven deacon to be punished with six lashes.

In 1266, St. Augustine's in Canterbury, due to sheer numbers, hired its own barber to efficiently shave its monks. Frequently, the first shaving of a brother in holy orders was an occasion for much cele-

St. Benedict Angelico.

bration and ritual. Specific prayers were written which commented on the hair's consecration on the altar, i.e., "Pour forth O Lord thy benediction upon him, let it flow over his head and beard, like ointment." The monk or priest renounced his locks and virile countenance in a symbolic castration as he gave himself over to God and his community.

One noted exception among the religious were the Franciscans, who chose to grow out their beards, a practice for which they are still known. They were different from Crusaders, who generally recognized that religious preaching to Saracens, or whoever had duties in the east and in the Holy Land, would be allowed to maintain their facial hair so as to blend into these communities. Reynolds tells an interesting story from the 11th century of a lay man who presented himself as clean-shaven when tried for robbery. Although he was acquitted for the actual theft, he was condemned for having the audacity to shave off his beard, something allowed only his spiritual superiors. (If you recall, the 11th century brought a dozen or so religious edicts against beard growth and the hairy schism between the Roman and Eastern Churches.)

In the life of St. Macarius, there is the story of two boys, one who wore a beard and the other who didn't. The shaven boy was plagued by flies who were agents of the devil and, because he was not bearded, had direct access to his unprotected face and soul. In the 12th century, the Abbot of Bellevaux wrote a tract called *The Apologia de Barbis*. In it he explained that the beard served to distinguish one sex from the other, and that it was natural to grow one. But somewhat less comprehensible was his argument that if we think of the head of the Church as Christ, the Holy Spirit "moved down from the head to the beard." He added that beards indicated strength and bravery, and that they became a pure white colour in the afterlife.

In the 16th century, a group of French priests in Toulouse were forbidden to wear beards under an Act of Parliament. Many priests got around this edict because of a subtle linguistic distinction: the French verb *porter* could be interpreted as either to wear or to carry. As a result, many clever clergy had someone else carry their beard so as to comply with the letter, if not the spirit, of this new regulation. From this point on, the beard became a Protestant trapping worn as a protest against the excesses of the

Christlike in my behaviour
Like every good believer,
Imitate the saviour
And cultivate a beaver

– Aldous Huxley

CHRIST BLESSING BREAD AND

Jesus.

Catholic Church, whose clergy had started to shave again (and still do, for that matter).

Over in America, a couple of devout Christians were persecuted for wearing their beards. Joshua Evans, an 18th-century New Jersey Quaker, looked down on shaving as an act of pride, and quoted the Old Testament frequently regarding his interpretations of instructions to wear a beard. (The Society of Friends, a pacifist sect, embrace the partial-beard.) He also chose to be a vegetarian, and refused to wear leather or dyed clothes. He kept his beard despite multiple protestations from his fellow New Jerseyites, and was restricted from travel by elders for a period of fourteen years.

Joseph Palmer, a contemporary who lived in Fitchburg, Massachusetts, proved even feistier. He proudly sported a beard, which drove his neighbours to complete distraction. He was told several times by his church community to remove it, which he steadfastly refused. In retaliation, he was reprimanded in a church service and refused communion. At one point he was even attacked in the street by four men with knives, but fought them off successfully with his penknife. He was arrested, convicted for assault, and thrown into jail, where he wrote letters of protest to newspapers across the country, further embarrassing his community. When it was decided that he should be released from prison, he refused, until forcibly removed. The whole affair is sadly ironic, because within twenty years, beards became universally vogue amongst Victorians and their American contemporaries.

Another bearded Christian sect is the Amish, the followers of Jakob Ammann. Ammann provided them with specific instructions regarding such practices as washing their feet and trimming their beards, among others. Primarily members of the old order of the Amish Mennonites,

The Lord God has opened my ear, and I was not rebellious, I did not turn backward. I gave my back to those who struck me, and my cheeks to those who pulled out the beard; I did not hide my face from insult and spitting.

– Isaiah 50:6 (beard-pulling as insult)

Amish man. *Galen R. Frysinger.*

they first moved from Europe to North America in 1720, with additional migrations following in the 19th and 20th centuries. The Amish settled in a wide area of North America that includes Pennsylvania, Ohio, Indiana, Illinois, Iowa, Nebraska, Kansas, and Ontario. Known for steadfastly adhering to their traditional ways, Amish men continue to be noted for their broad-rimmed black hats, their homemade clothes with hooks and eyes but no store-bought buttons, and their characteristic beards without moustaches. In some Amish communities, such a beard also indicates that a man is married.

HINDUISM/BUDDHISM AND OTHER SPIRITUAL TRADITIONS

Although it is noted that the moustache in particular remains enormously popular among Indian men, a trend quite unchallenged by time, no precise Hindu or other sectarian doctrine leaves instructions regarding its growth or maintenance. The moustache may be more of a patriarchal than religious symbol. Although gods were most often clean-shaven, it is noted that Ascetic generals grew their beards and moustaches as a sign of complete devotion and non-attention to worldly matters in their roles as mendicants and spiritual exemplars. The young Buddha is often portrayed wearing a moustache.

Some of the other sacred books of India do comment selectively on the use of razors: "In the beginning, Savitar, the Knowing One, shaved the beard of King Varuna and King Soma." Barbers were sometimes paid steep fees, like a car or an ox, if the client was a *Brahmin* (priest). Ceremonial shaving was seen as an act of purification by the devoted.

Then Job arose, tore his robe, shaved his head, and fell on the ground and worshiped. He said, "Naked I came from my mother's womb, and naked shall I return there; the Lord gave, and the Lord has taken away; blessed be the name of the Lord."

— Job 2:20-21
(shaving as starting over)

This religion originated in Africa, but its devotees mostly reside in Jamaica. Rastas believe that deceased Ethiopian Emperor Haile Selassie is the living God of the black race (though he himself was a Christian quite indifferent to all the attention); it is believed he assists them in battling white oppression as they plan a return to the homeland. Dietary restrictions are outlined alongside the use of herbs including ganja (marijuana) to purify the body. The dreadlocks of the Rasta symbolize his roots, his links to the lion of Judah, and radically contrast the straight hair of the white man. In defense of their beards, Rastas also cite Leviticus and grow them unmarred as an act of devotion.

✤ *Chapter 6* ✤

THE FEMININE BEARD

With few exceptions, facial hair on women has been the object of both neglect and scorn over the ages. No historic edicts, laws, or papal decrees have ever governed its growth, due mostly to the scarcity of the female beard. In modern times, this lack of attention may be explained by the relative invisibility of women, hirsute or otherwise, in political and Church hierarchy. Short of a few postiche-donning Egyptian queens, there are few examples of female facial hair that have been construed as powerful. When detected, the beard or moustache has generally transformed its female wearer into a witch, freak, or damaged specimen in desperate need of medical attention. Dr. Maureen Fitzgerald, Director of Sexual Diversity Studies at the University of

In the U.S., 92 percent of women shave their legs, 58 percent pluck their eyebrows, and 2 percent even depilate their toes.

Members of the band Maow wearing facial hair. *Paul Clarke/Mint Records.*

Toronto, explains that these adverse reactions hinge on a flawed notion of dimorphism — that body parts, genders, and desires exist as distinct opposites: "You're either this or you're that. We're made uncomfortable by people who remind us that all of these things actually exist along a continuum. Many men don't like the idea that all fetuses are female until a surge of testosterone gets the Y chromosome to express a boy. Similarly, if you are a male turned on by a bearded lady, you have to acknowledge incongruity and maybe even homoeroticism — it's much easier to turn her into something anomalous."

Not surprisingly, a very early industry of potions, creams, and implements sought to eradicate what is now called "unwanted hair." After all, women were meant to be soft, pale, and smooth of face in order to please their men who got to wear the beards in the family. Ironically, many so-called modern methods of epilation still require a rather high pain threshold, usually considered a male trait (particularly among those who think childbirth is a piece of cake). I was intrigued to find a small cohort of brave women in legend and mythology who grew beards out of sheer piety, sexual purity, or fidelity, and who were even celebrated for it. Galla, the daughter of Symnachus, grew a beard as a sign of uncommon sanctity. Phaethusa of Abdera pined out of love for Pytheus and grew a beard in his memory. (Hippocrates later believed that passionate love could turn women into men — this may have been an example.) A bearded Aphrodite was worshipped by the Pamphylians who linked her to the moon, which may explain the later witch-beard-moon connection in Wiccan history. Reynolds tells us that the women of Argos ferociously avenged their first husbands killed by the Spartans; as if that weren't enough, when they remarried, they wore false beards on their honeymoons to further prove that their love was worthy of men. (Amazingly, the new hubbies were not scared out of the boudoir.) Friga, a Teutonic equivalent of Venus, was an

Nay, faith, let me not play a woman; I have beard coming.

— William Shakespeare, *A Midsummer Night's Dream*

The bearded woman Hatshepsut.

hermaphrodite with a long beard; annual festivals in which men dressed as women and women sported beards lavishly celebrated her tradition.

One of the more interesting and enduring stories manages to capture elements of bravery, devotion, virginity, sanctity, and despair in one fell swoop. In one version, St. Kummernus ("kummer" meaning sorrow) of the Austrian Tyrol was a particularly pious Christian girl. When her father sought to marry her off to a neighbouring heathen, she grew a beard as a visible sign that she belonged exclusively to God. Her furious father had her killed, but her intercession was known to be powerful for young women in trouble. Another version tells of Wilgefortis, a 9th-century Portuguese saint. She too wanted to remain a virginal bride of Christ, so when her father, the King of Portugal, betrothed her to the King of Sicily, she prayed for a solution which came by way of a rather unappealing beard. Her father had her crucified for being such a bother. In England, she is known as St. Uncumber and her intercession in "unencumbering" women from difficult husbands was prayed for as late as the 16th century.

St. Uncumber's origins may actually be tied to lore around a cult of Cyprean hermaphrodites, and later to rumbling but enduring rumours of crucified women. A British psychiatrist recently offered a different take, suggesting that Uncumber, like many upper-class, over-controlled, sexually ambivalent girls, became severely anorexic. Her excessive hair was actually lanugo, a fine body hair which grows to regulate body temperature as weight drops perilously low in women with eating disorders. Uncumber was more neurotic than saintly, and killed off her femininity (self-castration) rather than become a full-grown woman.

Memorial statues honouring these hirsute girl-saints sprouted all over Europe. Another legend tells of a poor wandering minstrel who, in hunger and desperation, prayed in front of one of these statues

Father's whiskers grey
always in the way
Mother chews them in
her
sleep
thinking they are shred-
ded wheat.

– Anonymous

fashioned out of gold. To his surprise and relief, the statue helpfully kicked off one of her shoes, which the musician promptly took to a goldsmith for pawning. The goldsmith grew suspicious and caused a scene in the town square until a wise hermit suggested that the minstrel serenade the statue for the other shoe, this time in view of all. The poor man did this to the point of collapsing when all of a sudden the statue indeed kicked off her other shoe. The townsfolk were suitably chastened and the musician blessed for his devotion and persistence.

Anonymous bearded lady, 19th century. *Corbis.*

A quick survey of the historical European record of bearded ladies reveals quirky but not very useful information, mostly attesting to why women should not have facial hair. Voltaire chauvinistically suggested that, "Ideas are like beards. Children and women seldom have them." Early anthropologists offered that cavemen needed facial hair to brave the elements, while women minded the cave and remained smooth. (Clearly, testosterone had yet to be discovered.) In Shakespeare's *Macbeth*, Banquo comes across the Bubble-Toil-Trouble set of witches and utters, "You should be women and yet your beards forbid me to interpret that you are so." Royal patronage was occasionally proffered to a bearded woman — the furry Helena Antonia was beloved by Margaret of Austria (later Queen of Spain), and the hirsute Margaret of Parma became a Regent of the Netherlands. In the 19th century, bearded ladies in general made a big society comeback, but often under the unscrupulous direction of fathers, husbands, and tutors, and in the uneasy setting of travelling roadshows. In the early 1870s, P.T. Barnum founded his "Museum, Menagerie, and Circus," which evolved

World's Longest Female Beard: According to the *Guinness Book of World Records*, in 1884, American bearded lady Janice Deveree's beard was fourteen inches long.

into the enormously popular phenomenon called the sideshow. In France, one of the first famous bearded ladies was Clementine Delait, who was born in Thaon-les-Vosges in 1865. Being hirsute from an early age, she simply shaved until she and her husband visited a travelling circus. On spotting an inferior specimen of a hairy gal, she decided she could do better; she grew back her beard and joined a touring troupe. After becoming famous, she renamed the café she and her husband had been running as the Café de la Femme à Barbe; it became an immensely popular tourist attraction. Madame Delait continued her successful touring throughout Europe even after the death of her husband.

Magdalena Ventura de los Abruzos, a bearded woman, is depicted in a painting by Jusepe de Ribera. *Museo Hospital de Tavera.*

Another French woman, Fortune Clofullia, worked for P.T. Barnum and often performed with her son, dubbed the Infant Esau (a biblical reference) because of his pointy beard and considerable body hair. She was born in Switzerland and was managed by her father until she married her painting instructor. (I find it a nice touch that Fortune was schooled in the ladylike arts of watercolour and embroidery.) The couple moved to New York, where eventually she started working for Barnum. Once, a disgruntled circus customer accused her of being a fake and even took her and the circus to court; she prevailed, and the whole matter of course generated what P.T. Barnum loved most — controversy and free advertising.

Unfortunately, not all bearded ladies lived such happy lives. One heart-wrenching tale involved Lady Olga, born Jane Barnell in North Carolina. Hairy by the age of four, her unsympathetic mother took her to see the visiting West Orient Family Circus and simply left her there. When her father tried to reclaim Jane, the circus had already left for Europe. Later, when Jane became severely ill with fever on the road, she was abandoned again in an orphanage abroad. Her frantic father tracked her down and had the sense to place her in the care of her grandmother back in the U.S. (rather than his nasty wife), where she became a diligent shaver. As fate would have it, one of her neighbours had been a circus strong-man and managed to convince her to regrow her beard. She left with him at age twenty-one to join the circus as Princess, or the Lady Olga, where she was finally able to come to terms with her life as a bearded lady.

Annie Jones, Barnum's bearded lady c. 1879, at age 18. *Charles Eisenmann CDV, New York.*

Even worse is what happened to Julia Pastrana, who was born in Mexico in 1832. Apart from being short (four feet, five inches) she had large, odd teeth, a big nose and ears, and her body was entirely covered with black hair. She hooked up with a Svengali of a manager named (forebodingly) Lent, who eventually married her. When she died at twenty-eight while giving birth to a hairy infant, Lent had her body mummified so that he could continue to exhibit mother and child, at great profit, for many years. People simply couldn't get enough of it — death and gender transgression were dispatched in one fell swoop.

Another tale of woe belongs to Annie Jones, who was born in 1865 in Virginia, with both long hair and a significant beard. P.T. Barnum, who had scouts everywhere, heard about the child and convinced Annie's mother to bring her to New York. Once Mrs. Jones was convinced to exhibit her remarkable daughter, she devotedly remained in New York with Annie despite having six other children at home. All was well until an emergency in Virginia obliged her to return

Courtesy of Maggie Ross, MRI 2K.

Portrait of a Drag King

On a trip to Winnipeg, Manitoba, I came across a fine, locally produced calendar of drag kings in a bar called Ms. Purdy's. A few calls later, I was in touch with a star king who, as Carlos Las Vegas, has toured the U.S. and Canada and appeared on various TV talk shows. Carlos (a.k.a. Clarissa "CJ" Lagartera, a queer activist and university sociology student) explained that a drag king is defined as a woman who displays or portrays a physical interpretation of masculinity. The transfor-

south; she left Annie in the care of a phrenologist named Wicks, who promptly disappeared with the child. (Phrenology is a pseudo-science linking the bumps on one's skull to personality — we have it to thank for the distinction between "high-brow" and "low-brow" pursuits.) When they were tracked down six months later, Wicks insisted that Annie was his, until a wise judge, in King Solomon-like fashion, on seeing the mother's agony, sorted the matter out as to who really loved the child and returned Annie to her mother. Annie, who was known to be well-read and played the mandolin, eventually married twice — once to a banker and then to a wardrobe manager, with whom she travelled Europe.

Another American, Grace Gilbert, was born in 1880 in Michigan, completely covered with red hair. She worked for the Barnum and Bailey Circus as the Female Esau and Wooly Child. It has been said that in addition to being lady-like and good at stitching lace, she also enjoyed pitching tents while on the road.

The history of bearded ladies brings us to modern times. Jennifer Miller, a bearded woman profiled in a wonderful documentary called *Hair, There and Everywhere* by Vancouver producer Penny Wheelwright, works as a "postmodern performance artist" in her own Circus Amok. In the film, she speaks of the pleasures of wearing a sexy evening gown while sporting her thick dark black beard without a single trace of regret, stigma, or shame. Clearly, she has come to see her growth as something which distinguishes her and has helped her earn a living on her own terms. In the same film, Toronto's Keltie Creed talks about her beard and her painful decision to shave it off to accommodate her workplace. She was also told by relatives never to return unepilated to her grandmother's hometown, for having revealed the dark genetic secret of her family's bearded women. When she shaved off her beard, she describes the loss as greater than that she experienced at the end of a seven-year relationship with her girlfriend.

The trend to medicalize hairy women began in the 19th century. In 1857, an article entitled "A Short Account of the Hairy and Bearded Female" appeared in *The Lancet*, a prestigious medical journal. The phenomenon, or rather, symptom, became known as "hypertrichosis" and "hirsutism," another entity to be diagnosed and treated. Although ten percent of women have what they themselves deem to be excessive facial hair, normal familial and cultural variations are noted, especially among women from the Mediterranean. Menopausal women also tend — to their chagrin — to sprout chin tufts due to hormonal changes. Over the next 100 years, key pathological states responsible for "abnormal growth" were identified; a recent issue of *Merck Manual* mentions adrenal virilism, *basophilic adenoma* of the pituitary, ovarian tumors, *porphyria cutanea tarda*, and effects from drugs such as androgens, corticosteroids, cyclosporine (for cancer), and Minoxidil (a blood pressure medication which, because of its side effect of hair growth, has been reissued and rechristened as Rogaine for baldness). One final, fairly common cause of marked body and facial hair growth on women is called Stein-Leventhal syndrome (or polycystic ovarian disease). This condition consists of menstrual irregularities, weight gain, acne, baldness, and infertility, but is most often diagnosed because of the appearance of a moustache. I was surprised to discover how many support networks and websites, including chatlines, exist for the medically hairy gal.

A HISTORY OF ERADICATION

Attitudes toward female facial hair can perhaps best be tracked by reviewing the tortuous means women have used to get rid of it. A depilatory made of arsenic existed as early as 4000 BC. Five hundred years later, tweezers emerged in Mesopotamia, though clam shells had already been

mation can include several forms of body modification (i.e., removing long hair, wearing specific costumes, binding the breasts, and applying facial hair). The choice of facial hair, how it is applied, and its styling, ultimately enhances a king's persona. For example, a king may apply a stereotypical "machismo" or Latin look by applying a thinner moustache, with perfectly sculpted sideburns and matched with a goatee. Whatever the motivation, the application can certainly be challenging, particularly for novice drag kings (and those with sensitive skin).

For CJ, the preparation and application of facial hair is a kind of art form, and through trial and error, a fundamental and necessary skill. "It's part of the drag king-body-modification process and a kind of rite of passage to 'kinging.'" As with many drag kings, her moustache and burns are made of clippings from her own head — hair carefully repurposed for realistic effect. "Some kings choose not to use facial hair, but for others like myself, it completes the character that is portrayed on stage. Facial hair also helps accentuate the masculine features on the face, such as the jaw line, and at the same time it draws away from the more feminine features like the cheek bones. Us kings, however, have to be careful, as the simple gesture of a greeting kiss may render excess facial hair on some unsuspecting fan! You need knowledge in order to make the application look presentable or 'passable.' Therefore 'passable' facial hair application requires the study of men — how their hair or beard lies, where it begins, where it ends, how thick, how long. I

used for plucking. Roman women by 500 BC scraped off unwanted hair with sharp pumice when not employing razors and a cream made of byronia; by 400 BC, Indian women singed hair off with a lamp. Nero's wife Poppaea (4-68 AD) concocted industrial strength hair removers from lye, pitch, powdered viper, and bat's blood. Over time, an Arab tradition of using wax to pull off all facial and body hair from brides before their honeymoons no doubt added considerably to the erotic festivities. Odder trends emerged in the Middle Ages, when eyebrows and hair on the temple and forehead were plucked to allow room for elaborate headdresses. Elizabethans favoured extraterrestrial-like high foreheads with no eyebrows. By the 1770s, their French counterparts shaved their entire heads so they could wear powdered wigs; they also sported tiny eyebrow-wigs made from mouse hair.

In the 18th century, homemade hair-removal tonics were made from egg-shells, cat's dung, and vinegar, guaranteed to keep unwanted hair (and, no doubt, potential suitors) at bay. By the 1800s, European women were told to drink oak and wine cocktails in a hot bath for the prevention of unsightly facial hair, and to rub walnut oil on their babies' foreheads to preclude unsightly growth. Their American sisters used lye until 1840 when a so-called Doctor Gouraud marketed a product called Poudre Subtile, "the long-lost recipe used by the Queen of Sheba herself. " By World War I and throughout the 1920s, hems on dresses rose and sleeves disappeared. Skin was in. This necessitated women borrowing hubby's razor, though Gillette had first marketed a women's razor, Milady Decolletee, in 1915. A clever executive at Wilkinson Sword boosted the market with compelling advertisements suggesting that underarm hair was shameful, unhygienic, and unfeminine.

There was no turning back — hair anywhere but on the head or around the eyes was public enemy number one. (Hollywood starlets in the 1920s took it further, plucking or shaving off their eyebrows and replacing them with architectural pencil lines.) The ever-popular epilator, Nair, was developed and released during World War II by Carter Wallace in New York. Wartime rations made nylons scarce, and something had to be done about all those bare (and hairy) legs. Nair was a big hit, even if the product's early formulation, calcium hioglycloate, smelled like rotten eggs. Neet, its French cousin, appeared soon after via import. In 1940, Remington launched the first electric razor designed specifically for women; versions became rounder, lighter, pinker, and "more feminine" to distinguish them from their roaring macho counterparts. By the 1960s and '70s, American feminists, lesbians, hippies, and Birckenstock-wearers rebelled against all this nonsense and allowed their facial, armpit, and leg hair to "all grow out," while their European sisters, who had initially resisted the pressure, gradually but sadly crossed over to shaving. In order to return women to the shaving fold, Gillette introduced the disposable pink Daisy in 1975; the Sensor for women appeared in 1992, as women "came back to their senses." Shaving foams gave way to gels with fruity or floral scents instead of the more masculine mint or lime. The year 2001 saw the release of Gillette's triple-bladed Venus, built with a grip handle suitable for the shower, and "comfort shaving pads" to prevent chaffing. In television advertisements it rises from the mist to the rousing old tune of "Goddess on a mountain top," like an alien, millennial flower.

While many technological refinements targeted the removal of body hair, facial hair was not to be neglected, especially since women have, more often than not, objected to shaving it off; bad enough to battle a moustache, but to have to remove it like a man added insult to injury. For many women, the need to shave the face clearly offended their feminine identification. In 1981, Sally Hansen introduced Facial Hair Creme Remover, a milder, more fragrant preparation

Courtesy of Maggie Ross, MRI 2K.

stare a lot at men's faces. At times my obsession with the study of men is taken out of context or even misinterpreted by the very person I'm studying, where I'm eventually explaining that I'm not interested in a date but just wanting to mimic their facial hair for entertainment purposes."

I was delighted to learn that CJ takes her gender-bending act to dimorphic extremes when the facial hair comes off and she appears as glitter-glam-show-girl Karmalita Las Vegas. Turnabout is, after all, fair game.

Nikola Tesla.

than products like Nair. Jolen Bleach was developed to knock the colour out of your moustache and thus camouflage it. Ancient hot and cold wax treatments had reappeared in the 1960s, but subsequent versions made the painful process much easier with numbing anesthetic creams, microwaves, strips, and sticky tape. Cleopatra was often invoked as a pitch-woman.

Whatever the treatment, and however painful, women were, and are, given the message that facial hair was hideous and needed to be removed. Scientists, doctors, and entrepreneurs have never underestimated women's desire, even desperation, to remove what we now call "unwanted hair," or the fact that each customer will feel obliged to do so repeatedly throughout her adult life. Dr. Charles Michel, an eye doctor, inadvertently got the electrolysis ball rolling in the 1870s when he treated patients suffering from painful ingrown eyelashes with a low-voltage current that released sodium hydroxide at the root of the hair, thus damaging or killing it. By the 1890s, Nikola Tesla used a stronger current which delivered heat to the follicule and cauterized it. Thus, diathermy/electrolysis was born. The process was medicalized very early. But after physicians stopped performing the procedure, "certified" electrolysis "technicians" came into being, conducting their business in white lab coats in confidential clinical settings. Women who needed their help, after all, had a dark, downy shame and had to come and go unobserved. Though effective, electrolysis was never cheap and thus suggested an air of upward mobility, not to mention state-of-the-art scientific savvy. Immigrant women flocked to these salons at great sacrifice to more closely resemble their smooth Wasp sisters (who had probably better concealed their use of the technology). Electrolysis went unchallenged as the technology of hair-removal choice until the 1990s when another invention was shown to have applications in the vanity trade — laser treatments. The *Wall Street Journal* reported that 1,500 Americans tried laser procedures for hair removal in 1996, 500,000 by 1998, and over one million by 1999. Although the Food and Drug Administration requires doctors to inform "patients" that the treatment reduces rather than "permanently removes" hair, increasing numbers of women (and now men) flock to the magic light.

Another development in the history of facial hair removal is one of my favourites. In 2001, Vaniqa cream, a growth arrester, was launched with great fanfare in women's magazines. Its main ingredient, eflornithine, had been used until 1994 to treat the second deadly phase of sleeping sickness carried by the tsetse fly. More than 300,000 Africans develop the disease every year, and 55 million people in thirty-six countries are in peril of contracting it. Even so, at a cost of $700 U.S. for a two week course of eflornithine, its manufacturer Merrell (now Aventis) could not make a profit selling it to poor countries, so it handed the patent over to the humanitarian group Doctors Without Borders (DWB). How the drug was shown to eradicate women's moustaches is a mystery (especially since it was first invented to treat cancer). Nevertheless, with a potential market of 41 million women in the U.S. alone, an unlikely alliance between DWB, Gillette, Aventis, and Bristol Myers Squibb (another drug company who agreed to supply raw materials) was struck in due course. What's splendid is that while the cosmetic proceeds ring up, 60,000 courses of treatment for sleeping sickness will be donated for three years (and hopefully longer) to Africa. This has to be a first: vanity, profit, and altruism walking hand in hand in the wonderful world of pharmaceuticals.

Enough about eradication. The end of the 20th century brought increasing tolerance and even celebration of visible signs of gender-bending. We've seen certain groups of women and even a few celebrities who have bravely disavowed epilation of any sort over the years. A new generation of brave gender explorers even *desire* facial hair and the incongruities it suggests. Many menopausal women no longer pluck out chin hairs, but celebrate them instead.

There are some young lesbians who take androgens to encourage "secondary male characteristics" like muscles, deeper voices, and beards, with no intention of undergoing sex-reassignment surgery. Female-to-male transsexuals work towards beard growth as a part of their definitive treatment while their male-to-female equivalents, with their opposite yens, apply a product called Beard Cover to hide their dreaded five o'clock shadows. Drag kings — women who dress as men — wear appliqué sideburns, goatees, and moustaches, and have reinvented the idea of camp (see sidebar for a profile of one champion). "Chicks with dicks" — either true hermaphrodites or males with breast implants — generally present themselves as ultra-femme, but sometimes shake things up with a moustache.

Speaking of incongruities, a perennial favourite in San Francisco and at gay pride festivals is a band of nun drag queens called the Sisters of Perpetual Indulgence, who, in addition to their "bad habits," invariably wear cheeky beards below their wimples. I also recently came across an exhibit at the Tom Blau Gallery in London of photographic images of beautiful women with real beards. The Dublin-based photographer, Trish Morrisey, had placed an advertisement in London's *Time Out* magazine for hirsute gals to have their picture taken. The idea struck a chord with many of these previously stigmatized models. Morrisey, in an interview in the *Globe and Mail*, said, "I realized I'd hit a nerve while researching this body of work. Even among women who can talk very frankly about all sorts of other personal matters. However body hair 'where it shouldn't be' was something that was never mentioned. Women who responded to my advertisements were often talking about the subject for the very first time, and were very relieved and

somewhat proud to be taking part in this work."
Visitors to the exhibit reported feelings of puzzle-
ment, curiosity, and both lust and revulsion, but certainly not indifference.

If you are interested in more information on the
hirsute female phenomenon, enter "bearded lady" in
your web search engine. Apart from support-sites,
you'll be surprised to find a whole erotic world of
"hairy chicks" whose facial and body hair have been
fetishized (i.e., *www.hairychat.com*). A more playful, less
hardcore website offers a Hairy Babe of the Month
calendar — the brainchild of a Dutch Internet artist
named Jetty Verhoeff (*www.dds.nl/~beards/*). No longer
witches, saints, or freaks — these sexy women rock!

❧ *Chapter 7* ❧

THE UNCONSCIOUS BEARD

A man may profess to know what he's doing when he decides to grow facial hair, but if you ask a psychoanalyst, he'll tell you the man is wrong. The gesture of changing one's face is simply too powerful to be strictly conscious. The rather scant psychiatric and psychoanalytical literature available on the meanings of facial hair reveals that these decisions are based on notions of sex, death, aggression, rebellion, narcissism, damaged self-esteem, fetishism, and gender anxiety, and unconscious conflicts of the oral, anal, genital, Oedipal, and even vaginal varieties. Not surprisingly, if you think of each face as a unique tabula rasa, any attempt at adornment or disguise will be laden with meaning, both for wearer and observer. Such interpretations say much about prevailing taboos, not to mention religious, cultural, corporate, sexual, and political institutions.

Evolutionists have a more common-sense approach to why facial hair persists throughout history and what its enduring messages are. A beard gives a hominid the appearance of a larger jaw and highlights the teeth as potential weapons. Jaw-jut is apparently a universal threat signal in apes, very handy in set-tos on the savannah. We still value a big, square jaw in men today, though we believe it to be for aesthetic reasons rather than links to aggression. (Even the male peacock's elaborate feathers have been misconstrued as chick-magnets — they actually make him look bigger and meaner so he can scare off rivals.) Simply put, beards suggest power, dominance, and virility.

Evolutionary psychologists explain how we humans came to lose our thick mat of body hair, but soberly remind us that we actually have the same number of follicles as monkeys; our hairs are just thinner, shorter, and lighter. As apes evolved into humans, they gradually experimented with clothing, adornment, and fire, and thus required less dense hair. Armpits and nether regions of the body remained amply covered to trap musky secretions in order to attract mates, and in the case of the pubes, to protect and

The beard-wearer has clearly something to hide, even if it is only his weak chin and blubbery lips. A beard is a mask, by donning which the dimwit hopes to look like an intellectual, the penny-a-liner tries to look like a poet, the pavement artist seeks to look like a painter, and the bearded publican strives to pass himself off as a Merrie England Mine Host.

– Keith Waterhouse

cool the family jewels. Hair on the head was maintained to cool the scalp, reflect glare, and prevent sun damage. Our early ancestors may have preferred less hairy females, a trait which thus became selected and as a result persisted in subsequent generations. As males have always maintained higher levels of testosterone, they continued to sprout chest, leg, back, and facial hair — all serving to heighten their fierce appearance. Beards were also no doubt useful for obscuring facial expressions, which allowed for more subtle negotiation, and even subversion against the chief, when one decided to take on the top ape.

Anthropologists help us to look at the ritualistic and fetishistic uses of hair. Hair from the head, body, and pubes (sometimes alongside nail clippings) was ceremoniously burned or buried by early tribe members, lest it be carried off by the wind or animals. (Its ending up somewhere inappropriate was thought to result in nasty symptoms like headaches.)

Later on, witch doctors and shamans believed that the hair housed spirits; it was plucked for use in curse rituals, as well as to produce healing tonics at home. Elaborate rituals for burying hair in the garden or in holes in trees are described in the treatment of ailments, including gout and impotence. Young elite Delphians wrapped their first facial hairs around sprigs of grass to encourage fecundity, while Roman lads, witnessed by proud parents, offered their first shavings to the gods. Beginning in the Middle Ages, hair, mostly from the head, had been incorporated into rites of courtship and remembrance — your mother no doubt still keeps a lock of your baby hair, and your grandmother may have seduced your grandfather by sending him one of her tresses in a perfumed envelope. Such practices underscore the enduring symbolic meanings attributed to hair in its capacity to represent the essence of a person. But why does how we wear our hair mean so much? Of course, most of the reasons lie deep in our unconscious minds.

How many cowards,
whose hearts are all as false
As stairs of sand, wear yet upon their chins
the beards of Hercules
and frowning Mars,
Who, inward searched, have livers white as milk!

— William Shakespeare,
The Merchant of Venice

In the 1950s, Dr. Charles Berg, a London-based psychoanalyst, wrote a book entitled *The Unconscious Significance of Hair*. His treatise is dead serious, though I challenge the contemporary reader to get through my overstated version with a straight face. In Berg's view, hair on the face and the head displace endopsychic tension from the equally furry but anxiety-provoking anus and genitals, where, as everyone knows, everything really happens in our psychological development. Historically, or at least in Victorian times, these bits were rarely displayed in public (though for some reason we cannot stop doing so in modern times).

Sigmund Freud. *Library of Congress, LC-USZ62-72266.*

Berg reminds us that at puberty facial hair sprouts at the same time as pubic sprigs, signifying full reproductive capability, burgeoning sexuality, and male potency. All of this would be completely natural and fine if it weren't for the many who harbour old, unresolved conflicts about their parents. In Oedipal (Freud's) theory, some of us still want to seduce Mommy and to kill Daddy. Our emerging unruly beards become the equivalent of defiant erect penises, shamefully visible to all of society, which is why they must be cut down through the ritualistic act of shaving.

We may have worked through a thing or two by attempting to identify with our fathers (whom we have hairily come to resemble), but we still need to psychically castrate ourselves daily to reduce this rivalrous tension. We find it simply unbearable to flaunt our unresolved Oedipal conflicts on our faces, so we ease the pain with a razor, remaking ourselves through foamy (and, Berg would argue, spermy) renunciation. In Freud's triumvirate model of the mind, all grooming can be seen as a form of endopsychic compromise between the scissors-yielding superego, the hair-sprouting id, and the embattled ego which mediates between our inner worlds and societal expectations. Thus, shaving is both a symptom of and defense against id impulses towards our parents. The self would become a patricidal, incestuous, hairy phallus if left unchecked, so we kill it just to carry on.

The narcissistic pleasure we appear to derive from trimming, plucking, cutting, dyeing, and perfuming our hair diverts libidinous energy to love of the self. We also manage to control our other main instinct — aggression/death — by taking it out on our hair, which is dead in the first place. If we're lucky and all these defenses work, we can be at peace with ourselves, and even come to identify with benevolent bearded figures like God or Santa Claus. (Berg describes Father Christmas as a symbolic big cock, pulling little penis-gifts for good children off the big-phallus Christmas tree.) We project bad hair days onto evil figures like Satan and werewolves and historical person-ages like Rasputin, men who let their ids and aggression run wild. (As I read Berg's treatise it occurred to me that he never once mentioned whether women like beards or whether beards can get a guy a date.)

Santa Claus.

Our ideas about hair can also be plagued by pre-Oedipal con-flicts: infantile oral and anal striv-ings which weren't worked through early in life (or at least by age four). Their hallmark is a sense of tremendous neediness (think Pac-Man hungry), rage, hoarding, and exhibitionism. If this is your hang-up, wild, unkempt hair is like a dirty anus because hair now, of course, signifies fecal matter. We

Rasputin.

Then she said to him, "how can you say, 'I love you,' when your heart is not with me? You have mocked me three times now and have not told me what makes your strength so great." Finally, after she had nagged him with her words day after day, and pestered him, he was tired to death. So he told her his whole secret, and said to her, "A razor has never come upon my head; for I have been a nazirite to God from my mother's womb. If my head were shaved, then my strength would leave me; I would become weak, and be like anyone else." When Delilah realized that he had told her his whole secret, she sent and called the lords of the Philistines, saying, "This time come up, for he has told his whole secret to me." then the lords of the

can, however, expiate anal rage by cutting and shaving and getting to the salon on a regular basis. But if we go overboard in our defenses, we develop obsessive symptoms, such as excessive grooming, or using too much perfume or make-up to hide our unbearable stench. According to classical theory, in this phase we're much less worried about castration; our mother's (or society's) disapproval at our soiling seems to rein in most of us. According to this theory, those of us who persist in wearing messy beards may be truly without psychological redemption.

Unconscious explanations become even more complicated in cases of the sexual fetishization of hair, by no means a new phenomenon. Scalp hair is generally seen as a sign of genital vitality and appeals unabashedly to all of our five senses. If we haven't navigated the landmines of age-specific developmental conflict, our strivings to love, mate, and attach may become splintered and fragmented. We fall for a shoe or a wig rather than its wearer. We substitute fascination with what is called a partial object for the whole. We choose a symbol which somehow captures the person's erotic essence — a moustache, a plait of hair. Freud elaborated that men become fetishists because of an aversion to female genitalia. The woman's absence of a penis suggests that the Grim Reaper has already paid a visit, heightening the poor man's own castration anxiety. Much safer to fall for the locks on her head, as they are symbols of a restored phallus, geographically removed from the scarier bits. (I was delighted to discover that Charles II had no such conflicts — he routinely sported a wig made of his mistresses' pubic hair.) Berg even kindly codifies types and colours of hair for unconscious symbolism, so you know what you're up against:

```
gold = goodness
dark = demonic/libidinous
curly = pubic
fair = passive/clean
```

red = vulva
stiff = erect
soft = non-pubic

The early sexology literature recounts stories of men who sneaked up on girls and cut off snippets or pigtails (a symbolic rape), saving them for guilty onanistic pleasures. Though hair fetishes were seen as predominately a heterosexual expression, Krafft-Ebing, in *Aberrations of Sexual Life*, wrote about a twenty-year-old man with a moustache fetish. When the lad finally found the man of his dreams, the latter's 'stache proved to be fake, much to the chagrin of our subject. Havelock-Ellis later disputed the sadistic or aggressive motives often ascribed to hair-kinks, describing them as pure fetishes, linked to symbolic displacement.

Let us leave Freud and Dr. Berg to look at some other possible psychological meanings for sporting facial hair, maybe even a few that have been corroborated by research. As we've seen elsewhere, wearing a beard has always been an important visible signal of belonging or affiliation — Muslims, Orthodox Christians and Jews, Quakers, Sikhs, priests, monks, military men, and even a few psychoanalysts throughout history have identified each other and distinguished non-believers/non-participants through the presence or absence of facial hair. This was and is an extremely useful form of visual shorthand for building group cohesion, loyalty, and *esprit de corps*: you were in or you were out, and your allegiance to your leader included copying his appearance, as well as embracing his ideas. Beards have also been enduring, if temporary, symbols of grief, loss, bereavement, unemployment, and mental disorder in societies that insisted upon the stability suggested by shaving. As a result, what you were feeling was clearly written on your face for all to see. It's also fair to say that ever since Beau Brummell, modern societies have afforded males few expressions of vanity or creative expression with

Philistines came up to her, and brought the money in their hands. She let him fall asleep on her lap; and she called a man, and had him shave off the seven locks of his head. He began to weaken, and his strength left him. Then she said, "the Philistines are upon you, Samson!" When he awoke from his sleep, he thought, "I will go out as at other times, and shake myself free." But he did not know that the Lord had left him. So the Philistines seized him and gouged out his eyes. They brought him down to Gaza and bound him with bronze shackles; and he ground at the mill in the prison. But the hair of his head began to grow again after it had been shaved.

—Judges 15:16-22 (shaving as symbolic castration)

respect to their appearance, either in terms of dress or facial adornment. Fur fads have allowed such strivings to be explored in socially acceptable (i.e., "masculine") ways. However, given the revolving fashion of facial hair, what was improvisation or rebellion in one generation often proved to be conformity for another. Hence, the sideburns of the stodgy colonel in the Raj meant something radically different from those Elvis pioneered when he was all shook up.

One persistent association studied by the evolutionary psychologists links the beard and virility, and this has been tested in a number of experiments. A study published in *Nature* in 1970 showed that beards grow more rapidly when men are having regular sexual intercourse or — attesting to optimistic horniness — even anticipate such regularity. Psychologist Robert Pellegrini concluded in *Psychology* in 1973 that "the male beard communicates an heroic image of the independent, sturdy and resourceful pioneer, ready, willing and able to do manly things." He established this by hiring eight bearded men between the ages of twenty-two and twenty-eight to be photographed in various stages of facial display — with full beards, goatees, moustaches, or without any facial hair. These photos were then given to subjects to rate specific personality traits. Those models with the most facial hair were considered to be more masculine, mature, dominant, courageous, liberal, self-confident, intelligent, and healthy. (I have a sneaking suspicion that Dr. Pellegrini may have been a beardie.)

Other studies involving facial hair came to interesting conclusions. In 1969, Friedman had already determined that females found a bearded face to be

There Are Certain Days When Shaving Seems Like Suicide

I remember admiring my father's face
after each close Sunday shave
his adult throat
suffering the slits and slashes
of that outrageous morning's new blade
the sink water thinly juiced
with his slow-splitting essence
where cut hairs blinked and gathered
against the small skull islands of shaving soap
how he occasionally mended these nicks
with little bits of toilet tissue
epoxied to the flesh
by crimson clots
though one or two would drop
like rain-wet geranium petals
or later
when he would peel them
from his gullet
above the collar of his crisp white shirt

how he would well again
from the unstypticed wound

more sophisticated, independent, mature, and masculine, a finding which Roll replicated in 1977. Addison, in 1989, asked 114 male and female students to rate pictures of bearded men for characteristics associated with masculinity; although the hirsute were found to be masculine, aggressive, strong, and dominant, they were also seen as less desirable as mates. And in 1993, Terry controlled variables for eyeglasses, hair-length, and facial hair; and determined that the bearded were the least competent! These various experiments represent twenty years of studies, with conclusions very much determined by time and place; the '60s were a pro-hair period, the late '80s less so. Masculinity itself, indisputably symbolized through facial hair, is similarly seen to be valued then devalued, no doubt due to such social pressures as feminism, corporate expectations, and anti-militarism.

I was quite surprised that overall the opinions of women about beards were absent in most of the psychological and psychoanalytic material I reviewed. Surely a mate's preference figures into a man's decision to sprout or not. One 2001 web poll (sponsored by a hair dye company) found that seventy-five percent of women under the age of fifty approved of facial hair, even found it sexy, quite unlike their sisters interviewed eleven years earlier by Addison. Those who didn't like facial hair found it "dorky," "too common," "abrasive to the face," and "a desperate attempt at cool." I concluded that young women generally follow the prevailing zeitgeist, while older women overall prefer clean-shaven specimens. But even this consensus was challenged by a more objective survey published in *Men's Fitness* (September 2001). Here the

the tiniest pool of red
like an ink blot on a valentine heart
to which he would apply a kleenex corner
but if he forgot them
these rosy rags would ride his larynx
raised in church song
till my mother nursed them from their
station
like precious overseas postage stamps
careful not to re-excite the bleeding place.
Instead of God
I might sit and contemplate these
tiny puckered blossoms
where my mother set them on the pew
beside my sister's white communion gloves
stigmata on the blonde grain of the wood
the despair of flowers
fallen from the brief season of my young
father's grief.

— John B. Lee, *When Shaving Seems Like Suicide* (Goose Lane Editions, 1992); re-issued in *The Half-Way Tree: poems selected and new* (Black Moss Press, 2001), reprinted with permission

clean shave was preferred hands down by 97 percent of young women. Stubble and sideburns rated only a 26 percent full approval ("Yum") rating. The goatee came in at 20 percent, the full beard at 17 percent, the moustache and mutton chops at 9 percent, and the soul patch at 6 percent. The Amish beard was favoured by a lowly 3 percent.

M odern men seem to be sabotaging themselves if they think face fuzz will win them erotic points, since overall, women scored it as "yucky." So why do we cling to it so?

The answer is tied to the important developmental significance conferred to facial hair as a man navigates adulthood. The young teen wears his peach-fuzz as a badge of horniness, but is soon encouraged by parents to pick up a razor. His adolescent rebellion leads him to try something new — a goatee if he can manage it, or a moustache if his growth is patchy. He soon follows predominant college fads fuelled by imagery from Hollywood, sports, pop music, and pornography, all the while hoping to look older, "bad" to rivals, and attractive to mates. He enters the workforce and is obliged to tone it down until his status is secure, then he goes "bohemian" to prove he hasn't sold his soul and can still deviate from social expectations. As he enters middle age, he is unlikely to accept it lying down — if clean shaven, he may adopt his son's goatee. (How's that for rivalry?) If his beard greys and thus reveals his age, he may dye it or shave it off to look younger. If he has wrinkles or a double chin, he may suddenly go hairy instead of going under the knife.

The older man may maintain life-long habits, grow a full beard, or revert to the style of his carefree twenties as one last act of freedom. A good recent example of this transitionism is Al Gore. In the summer of 2001, the most famous near-president of the U.S. returned home from his holiday sporting a well-trimmed, full beard. His picture made the front page in papers across the U.S. and Canada and I was asked

Behold, Esau my brother is a hairy man, and I am a smooth man.

– Genesis 15:27

by National Public Radio in Philadelphia to comment on the former VP's new signs of growth. No occupant of the White House has worn a beard since Benjamin Harrison in 1889 and none of the current G7 leaders has any facial hair whatsoever. "Is Mr. Gore leaving politics?" asked some of the puzzled pundits. I had to say that Al's choice was perfect in that it seemed to poignantly illustrate so many of the reasons that men grow beards nowadays. He did not choose a goatee, so there's nothing faddish or desperate about his new look – and he grew it on a holiday, when relaxed and away from scrutiny. Many commentators pointed out that he had put on weight and that facial hair made him look a little less portly. He'd been teaching at Columbia University, so his beard added scholarly distinction while marking a life transition from would-be-president to private citizen. Whether a temporary or permanent move, he had changed and perhaps disguised his public face as part of his personal re-invention. Always the good boy with his eye on the prize, the clean-shaven, straight-laced son of a senator – Al was not permitted the all-out rebellious hair-growth of the '60s (or apparently any of the era's other excesses), though he did have a beard for a time. If we look deeper, there may have been tinges of bereavement in his expression, having lost his dream by a hair in November 2000. If beards represent a phallic expression of Oedipal conflict, Al was all the more virile, and had psychologically slain both his straightlaced father and his over-glandular mentor. If the voting public's associations to beards are negative (i.e., radical, fringey, leftist, subversive, hippy) – too bad. They will have to get over it by the time he runs for office again. A beard was good enough for Abe Lincoln (and Uncle Sam, for that matter), after all. As Mark Steyn (a beardie himself) wrote in the *National Post* – there will be "No More Close Shaves For Al Gore." If Al's beard signified a departure from political life, he had chosen a perfect symbol of freedom and may have unleashed a rash of middle-aged imitators.

Freud's Beard

Freud wore a goatee for much of his career, a style which was commonplace for European physicians of his era. I have a postcard of him which I purchased in Vienna at the museum located in his one-time residence. He is older here – his beard contains an elegant quantity of white and grey. His eyes are sad – too many defections, ideological schisms? Weariness from the daily act of listening? I find this picture poignant because Freud later developed jaw cancer, which meant that unbearable pain was concealed under that patient, wise beard. Freud's beard is perhaps the most famous of modern times – often stroked in caricature, much beloved, ironic in that all psychiatrists are somehow still expected to have one. It offered no protection in the face of death.

The decision to shave off long-cultivated facial hair is not one to be taken lightly. David Martin, in a *Globe and Mail* piece entitled "Saying Bye-Bye to a Very Special Patch of Thatch," lovingly tells of the moustache he tended and admired since he was in his mid-twenties. As part of a midlife crisis (after being told he might look younger without it), instead of buying a sports car or taking a mistress, he shaved his moustache off. He describes the experience as something akin to phantom-limb pain, and what I henceforth will generically christen "beard bereavement" (Martin cheekily hinted that he'd grow it back after he was over his crisis). Facial hair may technically be dead, but it's a lively expression of a man's personality (not just his conflicts), and it's clear that he loses a piece of his soul (not merely his phallus) when he shaves it off.

And what of the millennial beard? The end of the 20th century has seen the diminishing influence of the Church, psychoanalysis, and the military, and lesser preoccupation with social conformity and sexual taboo. This is the "Me Generation" gone wild. If hair is unadulterated bad-boy raunchiness — all the better. The modern man I've been studying on the street is blissfully unaware of — or at least disinterested by — the historical or unconscious significance of his current facial experiment. If ever relevant to his decision to grow a beard in the first place, taboo associations linked to desire for the mother, surpassing the father, lasciviousness, aggression, selfish individualism, Satanism, gender-play, homosexual signaling, grandiosity, or exhibitionism all appear irrelevant. Such motives, if at all present, are just as likely to be disavowed by our subject, exploited, or celebrated in zesty exhibitionism. Furthermore, if he has a mother fantasy, enjoys bearded ladies, or is a Satanist who is only turned on by men with goatees — there are at least a dozen websites for him to visit. There is conformity

El Diablo

Satan.

in rebellion, and uniformity in attempts at individualism — even your banker has a five o'clock shadow.

If you're plagued by trichotillomania (or obsessive hair/beard plucking), don't worry. Prozac will take care of it and your doctor won't even mention castration or anal messiness. Is the unconscious dead or just irrelevant now that sex and aggression are ubiquitous in the culture and thus seemingly less shameful? Do men need to continuously remind themselves that they are different from women in a post-feminist world? It's true females can now do anything men can do, but without hormonal help, the beard remains off-limits. I ran these topics, as well as those of Dr. Berg, by a gay-goateed psychoanalyst in a Toronto bar appropriately called Wilde Oscar's. I swear he stroked his beard as he thoughtfully responded to my questions. "The only thing you appear to have missed is the 'beaver' — you know, the vaginal beard." He went on without blinking an eye. "You know the type of goatee which circles the mouth and makes it look like a vagina? My take is that men with unclear orientation, as well as a lot of gay men, favour this style as an unconscious badge of femininity and submissiveness. Some secretly harbour the wish to be dominated or facially raped." An interesting take, at the very least. I told my friend Bert in London, a prolific gay sexual adventurer if ever there was one, about the vaginal beard. "Funny you should mention that. I was cruising a 'Bi-curious' phoneline and managed to persuade this Scottish bloke to come over. He wouldn't do much apart from jerky-jerks to straight porn but when he snogged my [hairy] face he kept saying — 'yeah, just like pussy.'" I'd had my comeuppance. Sometimes a beard is not just a beard....

❖ *Chapter 8* ❖

THE GAY BEARD

It's a few days after my discussion on beaver beards and I'm sitting in a café on Church Street, the heart of the gay village in Toronto. It's the first real spring day and short shorts and tank-tops abound; a lot of the bodies are muscular, epilated, and tanned, despite a harsh winter. What I observed earlier in quite a different context holds true here too: at least every third face, no matter what age, sported some form of facial hair. Men thirty and older seem to favour the goatee or circle beard while guys in their twenties sport other variants – fuzzy, sideburns, pencil lines, soul patches. There have been of a number of books recently interpreting aspects of the modern gay male body: *Gay Macho: The Life and Death of the Homosexual Clone* (Martin Levine), *Coming On Strong: Gay Politics and Culture* (Simon Shepherd, ed.), *The Arena of Masculinity* (Brian Pronger) and *Life Outside – The Signorile Report on Gay Men: Sex, Drugs, Muscles and the Passages of Life* (Michelangelo Signorile). All seem to suggest that an ultramasculine, commercialized physical aesthetic (what Signorile calls "body fascism") has spread throughout the gay community, demanding con-formity and often concealing internalized homophobia as well. How does facial hair fit into this picture?

Greek stamp depicting
Aristotle.

Historically, the beard, and later other forms of facial hair, have always figured heavily in homoerotic exchange, well before any construction of homosexuality as an actual orientation was ever articulat-ed. This bit of history is conspicuously ignored by pogonologists who, as I discov-ered, cheerfully document all other aspects of fashions and meanings of facial fur. Herbert Moller of Boston University tells us that there is considerable evidence that the onset of male facial hair has occurred at considerably younger ages over the centuries (averaging age fourteen in modern times). Its presence was enormously signifi-cant in ancient Greece, where Aristotle noticed that the beard made an appearance at age twenty-one, as "men go on increasing in vigour." Upper-class men unabashedly courted and loved beardless youth of the leisure class (showing no interest in prostitutes or slaves, who were beneath contempt), but only so long as their cheeks remained smooth. Parents and tutors shielded their charges from the flattering attention of

Leonardo da Vinci.

politicians and warriors. Even if the grown man's mission was accomplished, Plutarch documented the fickleness of boy-lovers who drifted away "as the hair grows." The sophist Bion wrote that emergence of hair on the face of the beloved ephebe freed the older man "from a beautiful tyranny." It was said that woe befell the adult male who amorously pursued boys after they had already experienced their first sprout of facial hair; thus, accusing someone of having such desires was the worst insult one could heap upon enemies. The lowly Macedonians, for instance, were known to enjoy anal sex with beard-worthy males, and this became one more reason to wipe them out. The scorn thrust upon any grown (i.e., hairy) man who enjoyed being penetrated persisted for centuries, particularly in Mediterranean countries; while the more sophisticated Spanish Muslim poets continued to pine and wax eloquent over milky adolescent lads. During the Renaissance, artists like Giovannantonio da Verzelli and Leonardo da Vinci (who maintained a fine, scholarly beard himself) kept inspiring, boyish specimens around their ateliers. We now think of Michelangelo's clean-shaven "David" as the epitome of such smooth, youthful beauty.

Meanwhile, throughout Christian Europe, same-sex love and eroticism were being driven ever further

A Timeline of Queer Facial Hair

Birthdates (*bearded unless otherwise indicated*)

495 BC
Sophocles
author of *Oedipus Rex*

427 BC
Plato
philosopher whose *Symposium* draws on examples of male love

418 BC
Epaminondas
Greek warrior

383 BC
Demosthenes
Greek orator

356 BC
Alexander the Great
Vain shaver

76 AD
The Emperor Hadrian
Roman Emperor and lover of Antinous who drowned himself at age twenty-one

1284
Edward II (moustache)
King of England whose first lover, Piers Gaveston, was murdered by barons; his second lover, Hugh Despenser, was castrated and decapitated while Edward was killed with a hot poker in his anus

1466
Erasmus (moustache)
Dutch humanist

1492
Pietro Aretino (above)
Renaissance dramatist

1566
King James I
King of Scotland and
England who was gay
(like his father)

1532
Etienne Jodelle
Playwright and member
of literary group La
Pleiade

1551
Henri III
French regent; gave
himself over to gay urges
as an anti-clerical act

1564
William Shakespeare
Playwright whose orien-
tation is unknown but
whose sonnets often cel-
ebrate love between men

underground. Revulsion towards sodomy was often articulated indirectly around matters related to facial hair — the man without a beard was seen as effeminate, passive, and untrustworthy. (As we have seen earlier, history provides ample detail of the beard as a much-required, enduring religious, political, and masculine symbol; intermittent exceptions emerged as a result of decrees issued by popes and bishops, who flipped back and forth in their interpretations of the beard and the razor, but clergy, whatever their real proclivities, were meant to be sexless in any case.) While men have always slept together, historically they have also conformed to cultural expectations around appearance, dress, marriage and, above all, the need to produce heirs. The notion of building an identity around preferred sexual habits, explicitly naming those habits, or rebelling visibly through style or a distinguishing signifier did not occur until the 20th century. If your confreres wore beards, got married, had children, went to war — you did too.

Smooth-faced, perfumed dandies and fops have always been ridiculed as effete, but aspersions on sexuality were veiled or absent so long as the love that dared not speak its name remained damned to hell and uninvoked. In Victorian times, Oscar Wilde changed all that in two ways. While everyone wore what he called "middle class" beards, he and Aubrey Beardsley remained shaven, flaunting outlandish wit and boyishly smooth cheeks. And, as is well-known, Wilde's activities with the young Lord Bosley were detailed in the courts in a most humiliating fashion on the instigation of the boy's father, which led to prison and death in French exile for poor Oscar. Alas, genius, style, and a clean shave could not save him.

If we consider the U.S., the birthplace of gay liberation, we see that over the last 100 years most men, straight and otherwise, have generally favoured the clean-shaven look. Early on, for men who loved men, this no doubt represented the necessity of blending in with general society, so as to be undistinguished from

Walt Whitman. *LC-USZ62-82781.*

straight peers who were also smooth-faced. (Some might call this a form of identification with the aggressor.) More recently, gay men came to fetishize the look of the young, athletic, clean-shaven jock and became obsessed with removing any offending body or facial hair that disfigured the much-sought-after boyishness. A gay cult of youth generally persisted throughout the late 19th and 20th centuries. One early notable exception was Walt Whitman — the earth father, man-loving poet who died in 1892. His paeans to beautiful youth were as unapologetic as his beard. (It's not generally known that he once met Oscar Wilde; in 1882, the 27-year-old "aesthetic singer" crossed the Delaware River to meet the "good grey poet" who was thirty-five years older. Apparently, they hit it off.) The woolly Whitman loved all shapes and sizes of men — young or old, smooth or hairy. In "Calamus 36," for instance, Whitman wrote:

> I now suspect there is something fierce in you, eligible
>   to burst forth
> For an athlete is enamoured of me — and I of him,
> But toward him there is something fierce and terrible
>   in me, eligible to burst forth
> I dare not tell it in words — not even in these songs.

In the 1920s and '30s gay men revealed themselves to be ever-careful groomers who occasionally sprouted Valentino sideburns or Clark Gable moustaches, as did everyone else. And like their straight brothers have always done, they sometimes grew facial hair to distract from a balding pate or double chin. By the 1940s and '50s, early "male" pornographers had obviously studied Greek history; their images of

Sir Francis Bacon (above)
English jurist & scientist

Corpus Christi College, Cambridge.

Christopher Marlowe
(above)
Playwright

1601
Louis XIII
French king and page-lover

1712
Frederick the Great
(moustache)
escaped his warrior
father with his male lover

1777
Alexander I (sideburns)
(above)
Russian czar

1778
Beau Brummell (side-
burns)
Well-sideburned fop

1805
Rufus Devane King
(sideburns) (above)
Beloved, sideburned
friend of bachelor U.S.
president James
Buchanan

young, smooth-skinned men wearing posing straps and cord-sandals were meant to produce noble recollections of athletic matches and displays of unrivalled strength. (It also provided an acceptable though titillating motive for these well-oiled models to grope, wrestle, and hold each other in post-battle exhaustion.) Jack Fritscher, a well-known gay author, reminds us that the corn-fed, baseball- or tennis-playing smoothie prevailed as a gay icon until muscleman Steve Reeves

Steve Reeves as Hercules.

burst out of his loincloth as the full-bearded Hercules in an extremely popular batch of B gladiator flicks in the 1950s. Men everywhere may have lusted after him, but very few followed his follicular challenge. (Poet Allen Ginsberg was a gay icon known for his lifelong beard, but his true inspiration for growing it is unknown. I see it as befitting the bard.)

By the 1960s, a New York-based homophile society (an early gay rights group) recommended the wearing of suits and ties and maintaining a clean-cut appearance in order to foster acceptance by mainstream American society. Members were accused by more radical elements of being unforgivable sell-outs — Uncle Marys and Aunt Toms. Meanwhile, hippie culture promoted dropping out, tuning out, and turning on. Flower children chose to "let it all hang out,"

which meant growing long hair, sprouting full beards and moustaches, and experimenting with sex (and drugs) of all kinds. Feminists and lesbians in the burgeoning women's movement fought the oppression of removing body hair, and many gay and bisexual men also subscribed to this compelling, free-love/free-growth ethos. By the end of the 1970s the Radical Faeries, a group of homespun, non-urban revellers, promoted communal living, pagan ritual, "gender fucking" (i.e., wearing loose dresses), and sporting proud minimally groomed facial hair as truly natural men. This predominantly queer movement, with ties to the non-macho men's movement, published a journal out of Iowa, called *RFD: A Country Journal for Gay Men Everywhere*.

Another key event in queer history took place in 1969, and facial hair figured prominently by dint of its absence. When New York police raided the Stonewall bar in Greenwich

Courtesy of Amanda McGowan.

Village, it was the heavily made-up, epilated drag queens who fought them off with feather boas and well-placed fists. Drag culture had been a source of underground entertainment for years, with its hyper-femme performers and outlandish carica-tures of celebrities. Although enjoyed by many gay men in clubs, drag has increasing-ly clashed with gay culture's mainstream push towards the exaggerated masculinity mentioned earlier. It has also engendered a persistent ambivalence towards the femi-nine. (Personal ads still often specify "no fems," a shocking example of ingratitude to historical forebears.) Quite ironically, in gay lexicon, "a beard" came to represent a woman who was dated or brought to social functions by a gay man, so that he could

1819
Walt Whitman
Ectstatic, man-loving
poet

1844
Edward Carpenter
English poet

Alfred Leete.

1850
Horatio Herbert, Lord
Kitchener (above)
English moustached
colonial and poster boy
for military recruitment

1853
Cecil Rhodes (moustache)
Arms manufacturer and
scholarship endower

1856
Sigmund Freud
Bearded founder of
psychoanalysis, once
wrote a compassionate
letter to the mother of a
gay youth

hide his true face, i.e., his homosexuality.

As early as the 1950s, pockets of exaggerated homo butchness and associated hairiness were emerging throughout North America and Europe. After World

Courtesy of Dave Mason.

War II, thousands of GIs who had confirmed their lust for men while in the trenches returned home, still very much influenced by military codes and rules. Postponed adolescent rebellion, combined with a parallel fascination with motorcycles and hitting the road, was simultaneously taking America by storm. When these desires coalesced, a leather subculture within the gay community was born. Gay bikers formed their own club culture, bonded by wartime memories, macho rites, and a powerful erotic fascination with black leather/denim motorcycle apparel. Sex between men was constructed as rough, ritualized, and focused on aspects of power and control. Sadomasochistic practices and role-playing flourished and became a new homoerotic norm. The look was hypermasculine — think Tom of Finland iconography — and both moustaches and sideburns topped (and bottomed) it off. (Beards, however, did not get incorporated into leather-SM culture or pornography, with any regularity, until the 1990s.) Leathermen became highly visible gay community players by the 1970s, alongside their smooth, muscular, often blond, Lacoste-wearing brothers. By the end of the decade, a hybrid (or spawn?) of the two became visible in every gay ghetto — the so-called "clone," with his short-cropped, military-style hair, obligatory

Village People.

Tom Selleck.

moustache, bomber jacket, beefed-up shoulders, and muscular butt under tight jeans. He was meant to be a working-class man's man, not an exaggerated caricature; or so the clone believed. The Village People burst on the musical scene, with *leitmotifs* of homolust at the "YMCA" or "In the Navy." The muttonchop leatherman and moustachioed cowboy became beloved by middle America, who had perhaps missed the precise erotic essence of such hit disco ballads as "Go West." The notably married actor Tom Selleck also typified the clone look in his *Magnum, P.I.* television series — perhaps another example of mainstream culture following and adopting an undisputably gay esthetic. It seems that every straight single-bar swinger in the seventies had a moustache and a hairy, gold-chained chest.

When HIV/AIDS hit in the early '80s, the clone look all but disappeared, partly because so many gay men were dying. Throughout the epidemic, a hard-hit community of leathermen continued to be hairy all over, but the only images in magazines and in mainstream gay pornography throughout the late '80s and '90s were of the baby-smooth "twink." Some authors believe that the shaved face, chest, legs, genitals, and anus on muscled bodies visible in AIDS-era porn somehow reassured men of the object's (or

Courtesy of James Johnstone.

Nadar (Gaspar Felix Tournachon).

1862
Claude Debussy (above)
Impressionist French
composer

1863
C.F. Cavafy (moustache)
Homoerotic Greek poet

1863
George Santayana
(moustache)
U.S. philosopher, poet,
and novelist

1866
Eric Satie
French composer,
famous for piano works

1871
Marcel Proust (moustache)
Aesthete and novelist

1874

Ron Suresha.

Carl Van Vechten, Library of Congress, LC-USZ62-42520

Somerset Maugham (moustache) (above) Novelist, author of the non-S/M classic, *Of Human Bondage*

1879
E. M. Forster (moustache) (above) Author of *Maurice*, a tender boy meets boy story

partner's) purity, youth, and by extension, freedom from disease.

Ron Suresha, a well known ursine observer and self-identified bear, interviewed photographer David Bergman for a wonderfully informative book on furry gay history called *Bear Book 2*. Bergman had more to say about the evolving meaning of body hair for gay men:

It's harder to photograph hairy bodies and get the same sort of physical definition. Light does not come off a hairy body in as photogenic a way as it does a smoothly oiled one. Then there are the class issues of thinness - the rich can afford the diets and exercise one needs to stay thin. But I think there is something else.

Hair is a deeply psychological symbol of both sexuality and mortality. Remember, Samson loses his power when he gets his locks shorn - and society in its attempt to control power wants to have us all shorn. But body hair especially is part of the abject - part of the dirty, smelly, detachable parts of the self that are associated with being mortal. And today especially, American society in general, and gay culture in particular, is torn by its feelings about its mortality. So along with the Bianchi models who look like marble statues, we also have the anorexic male models who look like they're on speed or heroin - gaunt figures of the nearly dead.

From the mid-'80s to the mid-'90s, gay men flocked to salons offering waxing, electrolysis, and by 1996, laser hair removal. One year, the company producing the hair-removal product Nair handed out samples before the Gay Pride parade in Toronto, encourag-

Courtesy of Alex Schell.

ing use by men so their six-pack abs and calf-muscles could stand out better. Gay men, like their long-suffering heterosexual sisters, had grown convinced that body and facial hair had to go if one were to achieve sufficient beauty to attract a healthy, manly mate. One researcher documented in the 1990s that facial hair was visible in advertisements and images in gay magazines like *The Advocate* only when products or services for depression, substance abuse, or HIV were being promoted. Little by little, personal ads have come to specify "no beards" in addition to "no fats or fems," as rampant beardophobia took hold.

Fortunately, by the late 1980s in San Francisco, men blessed with beer bellies, ample body hair, beards, and moustaches chose to hang out together in the Lone Star Saloon. They decided to celebrate their portly, hirsute habitus and to rebel against oppressive images of unattainable and arguably distorted physical perfection. In a move akin to feminists and lesbians disdainfully rejecting the pin-up as a body ideal to be achieved, these men adopted the bear as a symbol. This was said to be because bears are large, hairy, and strong (but also secure and gentle). Contrary to the cruising behaviour so often observed in bar culture, Bears prided themselves in being non-aggressive, non-predatory, loyal, and romantic (though I know a few "cubs" who would beg to differ). The bear movement was meant to be inclusive, democratic, and non-elitist in terms of looks or money. Bear-themed magazines and list-serves (cyber-dens) started to flourish in North America and then Europe. By 1987, *Drummer*, the magazine for leathermen (who continue

1880
Count Adelsward Fersen (moustache)
Swedish count who had a pink mass on his gay wedding day

1883
John Maynard Keynes (moustache)
British economist

1885
D.H. Lawrence
Bi-curious novelist

1886
Rex Stout
U.S. detective and western writer

1889
Clifton Webb (moustache)
Stage and movie actor

1892
Erté (sideburns)
Russian sideburn-wearing art deco illustrator

1892
Harry Stack Sullivan (moustache)
Distinguished American psychoanalyst

1909
Errol Flynn (mous-
tache) (above)
Sometimes-mousta-
chioed bi film star

1911
Tennessee Williams
(moustache)
Southern playwright;
author of *A Streetcar
Named Desire*

1926
Allen Ginsberg
Buddhist-Beat-
bearded-bard

1928
Edward Albee (moustache)
Author of *Who's Afraid of
Virginia Woolf?*

1945
Rainer Werner
Fassbinder
German bad-boy film-
maker

to see themselves as completely distinct from bears, because of more of an emphasis on musculature and SM sex), featured an erotic spread of "bears and mountainmen." Textual porn in bear mags and one-handed publications started to routinely fetishize images of ejaculate on beards, moustaches, and hairy chests, the feel of roughness on skin, and celebrated intergenerational attractions to hairy but maternal-nurturing Daddy figures (i.e., "then Daddy popped his load on my soul patch").

For many contemporary gay men, bears are still considered old, fat, undesirable, and on the fringe, but by the 1990s they had successfully reintroduced the sexiness of facial and body hair. When Colt Studios, the undisputed arbiter of homoerotic photographic male nude beauty, offered images of fuzzy, muscular, moustachioed men like Steve Kelso, the rest of gay porn followed both in print and in videos. As I had noticed while sipping my double skinny latte, urban millennial gay men, alongside their straight brothers, now sport endless permutations of goatees, soul patches, stubble, full/partial beards, and moustaches. Gay men, of course, insist that they started it, just like every other 20th-century male fashion trend.

But why now? David Graham, a fashion reporter for the *Toronto Star* who wrote a piece called "Pumped Up With Pride" just before the 2001 Gay Pride parade, has lots to say about the role of facial hair in the construction of the hypermasculine queer look so visible these days in urban centres:

> Once upon a time, gay men used to lust after straight, muscular, hairy, blue-collar types. Then it dawned on them that they could resemble such men by working out and dressing a certain way. They could actually become, lust after, and seduce that enticing icon.

Taken to the extreme, such forms of macho emulation can speak to identifying with the aggressor, doubting one's own masculinity, and even disavowing a more tender — dare I say, feminine — side. Such behaviour can also be an expression of internalized homophobia, where passing as straight is the ultimate goal. David tells us, however, not to belabour the last point — "A lot of men acquire muscles and facial hair to look tougher as a form of self-defense. You'd be surprised how much queer-bashing still goes on all over the world."

Although the bearded look may scare away potential bashers, it continues to be a signifier for gay men to recognize one another just like the rebellious long hair and moustaches of the past. A particularly popular style of late is the shaved head and goatee; the beard makes the face look less baby-like or lopsided. As one female friend said, "If his head is shaved, the haircut too good, or the goatee dyed or super-trimmed, I won't even try [because I'll know he's gay]." She had a point. David offered one last reason for the gay-facial hair boom over the last five years, something I hadn't thought of. Men being treated with the "cocktail" for HIV-infection often develop a medication side-effect called lipodystrophy, in which facial fat is lost, suggesting a drawn, gaunt appearance. "A lot of guys grow even, full beards to mask the loss of fat, so others won't know they're infected." We agreed this was another creative use of facial hair, but as if to avoid ending our discussion on this note, we concluded that, as always, gay men will continue to explore the tension between manliness and boyishness and will undoubtedly unleash the next great facial hair trend, whatever it may be.

1947
Elton John (sideburns)
Pop star who once used facial hair to excess alongside over-the-top glasses, shoes, and glittery costumes

1953
Freddie Mercury
Moustachioed glam rock star and frontman for Queen

1960
George Michael
Former Whamster; one of the first pop stars to grow a goatee (and variants)

❖ *Chapter 9* ❖

THE REGULATED BEARD

Just as I was starting to conclude that modern men have *carte blanche* to grow the facial hair of their choice, unencumbered by church or state, I ran into a twenty-something baker named Mark. He works in Ontario's cottage country and writes music on the side. The last time I had seen Mark he was sporting a very sharp blond goatee and moustache. But this time he was clean-shaven. I asked him what happened; he whispered that he had been told by his boss to lose the goatee "for reasons of hygiene." Mark suspected that some of the older ladies who shopped there didn't like it and "maybe found it a tad sinister." He concluded that he needed the job, so he shaved it off. I was suddenly entering the territory of the Regulated Beard.

It turns out that corporate head hunters and job recruiters routinely tell male candidates to shave off beards and moustaches before going for job interviews. Lisa Jackson, writing in the *Detroit News* in January 1997, acknowledges that outright beard discrimination exists, concluding that "some companies regard facial hair as non-conformist." In February 2001, the *Sunday Times* decided to test this premise and sent a reporter wearing a fake beard and moustache to interview for positions in several posh London hotels and restaurants. The response was overwhelmingly negative, and in many instances, the reporter was told that it was his beard that had ruined his chances, and it was suggested that he get rid of it altogether. Whether any of this is legal or not is a different matter, and in any case, at the pre-hiring stage that such discrimination exists is difficult to prove. Most private companies (as opposed to public sector employers) have the right to determine "the public face" they present to clients, and this may include precise grooming instructions for their employees. Sheri, a Toronto-based legal expert on workplace issues, suggested that it's reasonable to demand "that employees be clean, neat, and tidy." This would ensure that facial hair, if present, would be appropriately groomed and trimmed. She

I remember Drake, in the vaunting style of a soldier, would call the Enterprise the singeing of the King of Spain's Beard. (of the expedition to Cadiz, 1587)

— Francis Bacon,
Considerations Touching a War with Spain

added, however, that if an employer required all workers to be clean-shaven, such an instruction could amount to inherent discrimination against males. It might also impinge on the rights of religious groups who require the wearing of beards, like Muslims, Sikhs, or Orthodox Jews. She summarized, "Reasonable accommodations must be made for workers whose religion require a certain appearance." Even so, as I researched the matter further, I discovered the issue is not so simple. Several legal precedents suggest that restrictions may be justifiable if they are "reasonably necessary," for example, on the basis of health or hygiene concerns during food preparation. One example was described in *EEOC vs Sambo's of Georgia* in 1981, where a federal court concluded that despite a Sikh employee's protestation "to allow the bearded plaintiff to appear before customers, was 'undue burden' and might diminish confidence in the establishment's cleanliness." Another case against a large British food chain was similarly resolved in 2000. It seems that Mark was probably right not to put up a fight about his goatee at the bakery.

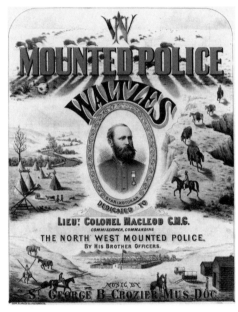

Cover of "Mounted Police Waltzes" (1880), featuring a bearded officer. *Glenbow Archives, Calgary, Canada (NA-2246-1).*

With the exception of food-related cases, occupational exemptions based on religious and health grounds often prove more compelling. In October 1999, the U.S. Supreme Court ruled that two Muslim police officers had the right to wear their beards unhampered. Both had worked for some time for the Newark, New Jersey force, which allowed moustaches and sideburns, but had banned beards in 1971. The problem came when in 1997 a new, zealous police chief promoted a zero tolerance policy with respect to facial hair. He permitted medical (dermatological) exceptions for the restriction, but not religious ones. The officers successfully argued that the policy violated their rights to freely exercise their religion. The Third U.S. Court of Appeals ruled that the two were indeed "entitled to a religious exemption since the Department already made secular exemptions." Disappointingly, however, in another police case in 1997, the Supreme Court upheld that the state of Massachusetts could continue as one of the seventeen states at that time barring facial hair on police officers because "the uniform code of personal appearance promoted esprit de corps." In another celebrated case in 1998, a U.S. firefighter, Brian Kennedy, won the right to wear a beard because the ban was determined to be a form of discrimination based on physical appearance. He may have been particularly lucky, because other precedents have forced even Sikhs to shave if having a beard would prevent establishing a satisfactory seal on safety or respiratory masks and equipment as are required in firefighting. (The Pannuh case in British Columbia was one such example; the plaintiff, who worked as a supervisor in a pulp mill, was expected to take a leadership role in the event of a toxic fume leak. However, it was decided that his beard would pose a risk to him, and then to others.)

Apparently in Massachusetts, an old ordinance declares goatees illegal unless you first pay a special license fee for the privilege of wearing one in public.

Regarding medical exemptions, several non-religious black men have argued the right to wear beards as the only clinical solution to *pseudofolliculitis barbae* (PFB), a bacterial and sometimes disfiguring dermatological condition which affects forty-five to eighty-three percent of black men, but only one percent of white men. Such an argument, called "Disparate Impact Race Discrimination," recently proved successful in striking down Domino Pizza's no-beard policy among its workers in the U.S.

I was amused to discover that an unlikely centre of facial hair discrimination — until 2001 — was Disneyland in California. Although Mickey and Walt both had famous whiskers, the theme park has had a no-facial-hair policy since 1957, two years after the park was founded. This reflected a time when the bearded were seen as bums, beatniks, or "sleazy carnies" who had tried to copy the Disneyland concept with fly-by-night carnivals. Disneyland was always meant to be the "happiest place on earth," where wholesome, squeaky clean staff served as role models to children. The policy extended to other Disney properties. In 1990, when Disney acquired the cruise ship the *Queen Mary*, several of its crew members were apparently sacked for wearing facial hair. More recently, for unspecified reasons, Disney held focus groups to discuss the subject; in March 2001, it was generously concluded that neatly trimmed moustaches were "consistent with what guests have come to expect." However, the rule still specified no beards, goatees, long sideburns, or body piercings. An interesting twist occurred the week after the updated announcement when it was determined that staff could grow moustaches, but only on their vacations, i.e., the workers could not have an unkempt appearance when greeting guests on the job. Many Mouseketeers felt this was a backdoor prohibition.

In 1999, the *Cincinnati Enquirer* reported a facial hair controversy in their vicinity. When the Cincinnati Reds baseball team chose to uphold a longstanding facial hair ban, the decision offended one of its star players, the goateed Greg Vaughan. The Reds were owned at the time by Marge Schott who was known to be rather gaffe-prone, and she held firm to the policy. The newspaper published over fifty letters of protest, many suggesting that the Reds would lose valuable players in the future if they didn't catch up with modern styles and changing times. "How he hits or catches is a hell of a lot more important than whether he shaves." Vaughan still has his goatee.

Also in the world of sports, a famous case in Canada involved Pardeep Nagra, a Sikh boxer who challenged the Canadian Amateur Boxing Association's (CABA) ban on beards on religious

The Specifics

U.S. Navy

- Sideburns must be of even width, extending no lower than the base of the earlobe.

- Facial hair is not permitted for midshipmen; neatly trimmed moustaches may be permitted, although these styles are subject to specific regulations by division.

- Sideburns may not extend below the earlobe; with a moustache, they may not extend below the line parallel to the corners of the mouth

- Officers must be "properly shaven" while in uniform: the moustache may not hang below the upper lip edge; it may not be longer than 1/2 inch. The face must be clean-shaven.

- With a medical waiver, officers may grow a beard 1/4 inch in length, which must be grown naturally and not shaped at the edges.

www.advancement.cnet.navy.mil/products/web.pdf/tramans/bookchunks/12470_ch1.pdf

U.S. Air Force/Army

• Moustaches are permitted but must be neatly trimmed and may not extend past the outer corners of the mouth, or hang over the upper lip.

• The face is to be clean-shaven; exceptions are granted with a medical waiver.

Air Force ROTC at the University of Maryland "Cadet Guide," p. 9

Canadian Armed Forces

• Sideburns may be worn, no longer than the base of the ear-lobe, and must be squared at the bottom edge. The length must be tapered to blend with the over-all length of the head hair.

• Moustaches are permitted provided they are neatly trimmed and not extending beyond the corners of the mouth. The face must be clean-shaven.

• Beards may be worn by individuals of Sikh faith or by men who

grounds. The CABA, in its wisdom, issued concerns that an opponent might be injured in the eyes by stubble — a beard-burn — or that facial hair might hide the severity of a cut. Although Nagra won a human rights appeal and court injunction allowing him to compete unshorn, the CABA responded by cancelling his weight division in December 1999, thus deviously sidestepping the issue altogether and upholding their most unsatisfactory position. Anybody watching old Hercules movies knows it wasn't his beard that clobbered his opponents.

The military in Canada, the U.S., and Britain — whether air force, army, or navy — all have specifications for facial hair. Some policies allow for medical and religious exemptions, but all are surprisingly similar in their instructions. The underlying premise seems to be the importance of maintaining morale, physical discipline, and overall conformity. Certainly the Emperor Hadrian's ancient suggestion that soldiers' beards could be grabbed in combat no longer applies, as *mano a mano* fighting is something of a rarity in modern warfare.

Happily, some millennial men have simply had enough with facial hair restrictions. A few Brits took matters into their own hands, literally, when they formed the Beard Liberation Front (BLF) in 1995. In 2000, they staged a beard wagging protest in London against "clean-shaven capitalism." One of their slogans is "to challenge the beardophobic assumption that beardies are weirdies." Apart from education and staging protests each year, the organization chooses a famous bearded man as a poster boy. In 2000, that individual was Frank Dobson, who happened to be running for Mayor of London against the clean-shaven Ken Livingstone. In March of that year, Dobson was told by his advisors to get rid of his beard; the Labour Party's senior pollster had consulted psychologists who suggested that bearded men are often perceived as untrustworthy. It was also felt that a clean face would make Dobson seem reinvigorated and more appealing to females and younger voters. Dobson essentially told them to "get stuffed," adding, "I'm not in the image business and what you see is what you get." He went on to become the Beard 2000 of the BLF, but alas, not the mayor.

Without a doubt, beards continue to be thought of as a liability in a number of professions. The majority of newscasters, delivery men, teachers, and salesmen are clean-shaven, but politicians are the worst off. For obvious historic reasons, beards are thought to be indicative of left-leaning tendencies, or possibly worse. This is quite a reversal from the 1800s, when a bearded politician was thought to be kind, paternal, wise, and virtuous. One rampant beardophobe was British Prime Minister Margaret Thatcher, who refused to advance the fortunes of any beardies in her administration; in 1985, 396 Tory MPs were clean-shaven. She was reported to have said that no one wearing a beard would advance in her cabinet.

One antipodeal politician who has taken on the red beard taint is Tasmania's Labour MP, Dick Adams. In 2000, he kicked off a campaign to end Australia's negative perceptions of facial hair. His grassroots movement, called "Beards Are Us," began when several of his constituents read advice about the necessity of shaving before applying for jobs, and turned to their profusely bearded MP Adams, who promised to "keep an eye on things" and to take on specific cases of discrimination. On his website, he predicts multiple court challenges over beard prejudice.

Meanwhile, early in 2001, the Equal Opportunities Branch of Britain's Home Office conducted "sensitivity groups" whose members were asked to note their "beardism" (i.e., beard-racism), or negative associations to facial hair. Although this was ridiculed in the press as political correctness gone awry, there is no doubt that people make snap judgments about their bearded compatriots based on old information, usually tinged with ethnic, racist, religious, classist, or even homophobic assumptions. Ask around and you

are unable to shave due to a medical condition.

www.vcds.dnd.ca/cic/cato-oaic/pdf/5504_b.pdf

Armed Forces: Britain

· Two styles of moustache are permitted:

· A neatly trimmed moustache that does not extend beyond the corners of the upper lip and that does not hang over the upper edge.

· A waxed handlebar moustache may be worn provided it does not extend beyond the corners of the mouth, and angles neatly upward. Its length must not exceed the uppermost point of growth below the nostrils.

· The face must be clean-shaven, excepting in medical conditions that prevent shaving.

British 1st Airborne Division Living History Association.

will find that Mark the baker was right — goatees are frequently associated with being sinister or diabolic. A chap wearing prominent sideburns may still be seen as rebellious, having a bad attitude, or being stuck in the 1970s. And a fellow with a five o'clock shadow may be seen as lazy, unclean, or a slacker. (People still haven't forgotten that in 1959 it was Nixon's stubble and bad suit that did him in when he was debating Kennedy on the first-ever televised U.S. presidential race debate.)

As suggested in the Dobson incident, a guy with a full beard may well be perceived as having something to hide, or being left-wing or a hippie hold-out. The moustachioed man may be perceived as retro, blue-collar, gay, militaristic, or "some kind of foreigner." These days, however, beards and moustaches are more likely to be a fashion statement than a sign of political protest, non-conformity, or religious affiliation. But it will take time for the corporate world to catch up. The current facial hair trend may have penetrated certain professions, financial institutions, and the high-tech world; whether it will become pervasive in the service industry remains to be seen. But we certainly won't be seeing many Western politicos, soldiers, or clergy with full thatches anytime soon.

There have even been recent setbacks. The Canadian navy was assailed in the fall of 2001, as the hazards of a 200-year tradition prohibiting facial hair were hotly debated. Once again the hubbub was due to the fit of fire-fighting masks on bearded faces, but as one sailor put it: "How am I to keep my face warm in a high wind in February?" The hairy dispute over naval beard banning rages on.

Meanwhile, if you're proud of your soul patch, attached to your sideburns, or married to your moustache, and your employer tells you to take it off, consider your rights. That order may be a violation of your freedom of self-expression, your personal privacy rights, your freedom of religious affiliation, your gender-specific choices, or ethnocultural parameters of dress. It will also help if you can get a doctor's note

Firemen are not allowed to have facial hair because it prevents breathing equipment from fitting properly.

A U.S. Marine's moustache cannot be longer than half an inch.

In 1936 Frenchy Bordagaray of the Brooklyn Dodgers was the only baseball player to sport a moustache and was ordered to shave it off by the team's manager.

proving that you require the facial hair to avoid a nasty rash. Contact the Beard Liberation Front or, better yet, form a local chapter. If all else fails, submit your tale of woe to one of the many beard and moustache discussion groups listed at the end of this book. They may have practical suggestions, but more importantly, they'll offer the kind of sympathy that only another beardie can provide.

❋ *Chapter 10* ❋

SUBSIDIARY GROWTH:
ALTERNATE FACIAL
HAIR EXPRESSIONS

Lest the moustachioed, sideburned, goateed, stubbled, and soul patched feel neglected by the discussion of facial hair thus far, this chapter is concerned with your iconoclastic history. In the

evolution of mankind, certain brave souls decided that you could selectively trim and shape the tufts that grew on your face, eschewing, as it were, the full enchilada.

I currently know only two men who wear moustaches — one is an older professor of psychiatry and the other is a French chevalier who works in ballet. For some reason, the 'stache has become an endangered species; one rarely sees them on the street, and almost never on young faces. But the moustache has a decidedly celebrated legacy. To me, the grandaddy of all moustaches was that worn by Salvador Dali. In photographs it stretches like a waxy tightrope and takes a sharp turn upward towards his crazy eyes and crowded thoughts. It's been said that

Zorro.

Salvador Dali.

in his poor student days, he actually used it as a paintbrush. It probably also inspired the hands on all those droopy clocks, too.

Details on the evolution of these *über*-whiskers is scant. For most of history, as is still often the case, the beard and moustache came as a single package, governed as we've seen by religious, political, class, and social convention. Even though for every male, peach-fuzz first appears on the lip, signifying the onset of manhood, boys have always been told to be patient and wait for the *real* thing. Somewhere along the line, however, someone had the idea to shave the lower face and leave the hairy upper lip untouched. As early as 2650 BC, Egyptian artifacts reveal men sporting a pencil-thin line — perhaps a chap's wish to look feline in a cat-worshipping cult — but by 1800 BC they had once again become clean-shaven.

Confucious.

(The anthropologist Desmond Morris tells us that twirling the moustache is an enduring form of male preening and seduction, but anyone who has watched cartoons featuring Snidely Whiplash or Dirk Dastardly knows that they do it when they have scheming on their mind.) Thereafter we see pockets of growth throughout Europe and Asia. In fact, a most scholarly moustache was sported by Confucius (b. 551 BC) and by most of the early, great Chinese philosophers who followed. Around the same time, Spartans exploited the masculinity of the moustache in their laws in that those convicted of cowardice had

half of their 'staches removed to induce public stigma
and shame. The Greeks completely disdained its
presence in the absence of the beard, while the
Romans cursed the barbaric Gauls, Goths, and
Franks, all of whom sported the uncivilized growth as
they sequentially plundered Rome. The ancient
Britons wore droopy moustaches, often dyed green or
blue, as an act of defiance against Caesar. By 200 BC,
residents of the Sarnath (thought to be the birthplace
of the Buddha) also wore distinct droopers.

Although the word moustache itself comes from
the Doric Greek, with Italian and French derivation
(*mustax* for upper lip), the Greco-Romans may have
named the moustache, but steadfastly refused to wear
it themselves. It took centuries until Charlemagne
(742-814) demonstrated unparalleled French chic
with his, while other Middle-Agers wore full beards.
The Welsh by the 12th century sang the 'stache's prais-

Peter the Great.

es as a sieve for drink (but any excuse to imbibe was likely sufficient). A few Normans (during the Conquest) and Crusaders likewise went beardless, but sometimes maintained the moustache. In the 14th century, the Black Prince (son of Edward III) is shown in portraits with quite a proud one. But inexplicably, in 1447, English parliament passed an act forcing men to shave their upper lips. Elizabethans similarly ridiculed the moustache as a sign of villainy and foppery (and, no doubt, Frenchness). Across the pond, Clemenceau and the wig-wearing Louis XIV had moustaches, but the latter shaved his off in 1680 when its greying betrayed his age. (Not surprisingly, by the 16th century, the clergy, who had long banned beards, had an opinion about the moustache matter: hair on the upper lip might trap the sacred contents of the chalice, so it was *verboten* for priests.)

Charles II (1630-85) consolidated a French connection when he maintained his suave, pencil-thin line, which many courtiers promptly copied. In the 17th century, Hungarians and the Swiss Guards were known for their trademark bushy lips, while in Russia, Peter the Great was busy abolishing beards and moustaches altogether (even though he had a moustache himself for a time). By the 1800s in England, upper lip growth was considered evil, almost a mark of the beast, this time because the wafer of the eucharist could potentially be abraded and damaged en route to the stomach. Various forms of moustache discrimination were promptly articulated (some of which persist today): it was believed that only fops, Latins, foreigners, infidels, those with bad teeth or unable to grow a proper beard would ever choose this lesser form of facial hair. In spite of such prejudice, both the beard and moustache flourished fifty years later in the Victorian era, even though Queen Victoria herself, true to the spirit of her reign, once made an unsuccessful attempt to ban the moustache in the British navy. The navy has in fact remained the undaunted domain of the 'stache ever since.

The moustache, quite as much as the beard, has a wonderfully powerful effect upon a man's whole expression. The idea of virility, spirit, and manliness that it conveys is so great that it was a long time the special privilege of officers of the army to wear it, as characteristic of the profession of arms. It has now become general in almost all classes.

– Mrs. C.E. Humphry, *Etiquette For Every Day* (1904)

Bust of Wild Bill Hickock. *John C.H. Grabill photo, 1891. Library of Congress, LC-USZ62-46192.*

Men with waxed moustaches, like Hercule Poirot's, sometimes sleep with a moustache bra in place to keep things in shape until the next morning.

A whole European industry of combs, brushes, waxes, pomades, oils, dyes, and hairnets burst forth to service the moustache (and beard/sideburn) revolution. Throughout the early 19th century, French militia men, the Hassars, and the Prussian guard all wore moustaches, firmly establishing them as *de rigeur* for all military men who were the fashion plates of their time. Interestingly, however, the King of Bavaria forbade his men to wear them in 1838, although this eccentric ban didn't last long. It was around this period that the Spanish came to proclaim in one of their famous proverbs that "a kiss without a moustache is like an egg without salt" (though Jean-Paul Sartre later changed it to "a kiss without a moustache ... is like good without evil"). Clearly, Spaniards and Frenchmen knew a good thing when they grew it. Meanwhile, in the colonies, spritely American men embracing dandyism in places like New York City sported fine moustaches. The Civil War saw the walrus and handlebars become popular on both sides of the battle. Later on, soldiers in the Mexican-American War, gold-rushers, and Buffalo Bill (with his long hair, 'stache, and goatee) contributed to the enduring frontier, wild-man iconography of the moustache. Three U.S. presidents (and none since) had them: Grover Cleveland, Theodore Roosevelt, and William H. Taft. In fact, Teddy's was about as bushy as it gets.

By 1872, a product which prevented food from being trapped in facial hair was actually patented, so ubiquitous were beard-moustache-sideburn combos. Moustache cups, with their porcelain edge for the 'stache to perch and stay

Theodore Roosevelt. *Pach Brothers, Library of Congress, LC-USZ62-13026.*

dry while a man drank, were issued in all shapes and sizes. They were originally invented in 1830 by Harvey Adams, an English potter who struck it rich with the concept. In 1902, another very popular product was the Kaiser Mustache Trainer, a German-designed contraption named after the much-moustachioed Kaiser Wilhelm II, with gauze, elastic, and straps to keep one's points reaching ever upward.

Despite the growing popularity of the 'stache, however, there were still sporadic movements against them.

George Bernard Shaw. *Davart Co., LC-USZ62-25210.*

In 1907, New Jersey representative Cornish tried unsuccessfully to introduce a tax on facial hair while promoting the moral virtues of a clean shave. In a similar vein, a rather famous British testament, that of William Budd, circa 1862, stipulated that his son would be completely disinherited if he ever dared sprout a moustache. Law students continue to marvel at the prejudice and unresolved "control issues" Mr. Budd inflicted on his progeny even after death. Even the furry George Bernard Shaw made numerous cracks about foreigners and dandies with moustaches: in his play *Pygmalion*, the character Nepommuck was "evidently a foreigner guessable as a whiskered Pardour from Hungary, but in spite of the ferocity of his moustache, he is amiable and genially voluble." Shaw was a full-beard man and probably had no use for lesser expressions.

By 1914 and the advent of World War I, the military moustache was well-established and pampered like an orchid — certain British regiments insisted on its growth and this period saw the toothbrush and handlebars become standard issue. Generally, the shape of the 'stache suggested rank: officers had waxed, pointy manifestations while

Cigarette package depicting moustachioed man. *Goodwin & Co., Library of Congress, LOT 13163-08, no. 6.*

Joseph Stalin.

Groucho Marx.

Clark Gable.

infantrymen tended towards the thick and shaggy.

The 1920s, '30s, and '40s saw the emergence of the moustache as a visual icon with distinct political and cultural associations that are powerful even now in our understanding of the modern 'stache. You already know who these famous players are: Charlie Chaplin grew his comical caterpillar, to be later copied by Hitler. Another despot — Joseph Stalin — is also instantly recognizable because of his upper lip growth, not unlike Saddam Hussein in recent years. Groucho Marx wore bushy eyebrows and a moustache that were painted on, until they became his trademark and he finally grew them in permanently. Chester Conklin's Keystone Cop walrus-style was a phony he kept in his pocket and pulled out when he wanted to be recognized. Other actors like Clark Gable and Douglas Fairbanks exuded impossible *savoir faire* and sex appeal with their thin 'stache styles.

The '30s saw barbers clip particular moustache styles and trim variants like the consort, shadow, guardian, major, general, military, coleman, and regent. The Fu Manchu movies of the period demonized a Chinese villain with a long, drooping growth (which has become a huge style today) despite the fact that the novels in which the character appears (written by Nayland Smith) suggest no such adornment.

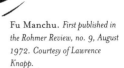

Fu Manchu. *First published in the Rohmer Review, no. 9, August 1972. Courtesy of Lawrence Knapp.*

Barber shop quartets, complete with straw hats, striped jackets, and, of course, classic handlebar moustaches, piped up with minimal provocation across the U.S. at county picnics. In 1944, an article in the *New York Post* described the "tidy" moustache-wearer as confident, dignified, and distinguished, and the heroic RAF pilots known as the Desert Rats were seen as dashing examples. In less macho camps, Salvador Dali and Marcel Proust grew unparalleled "artistic moustaches" and Agatha Christie's great Belgian detective Hercule Poirot was as noted for his upturned waxed wonder as he was for his snooping abilities. Albert Einstein with his frizzy grey hair and furry lip became the epitome of scientific genius. In the world of board games, which hit the market after the war, Colonel Mustard (of Clue fame) and the jolly banker in Monopoly managed to convey an avuncular quality to generations of game-addicted children.

Generally, non-celebrity 'stachers are a self-protective lot. In 1947, actor Jimmy Edwards formed the Handlebar Club in a London pub — a group of moustachioed men (absolutely no beards allowed) who met

David Suchet as Hercule Poirot.

Colonel Mustard from a
vintage edition of the
board game Clue. *CLUE® &
©2001 Hasbro, Inc. Used with
permission.*

Robert Goulet.

for monthly "sport, conviviality," and charitable works. Similar clubs sprung up across Europe including Germany, Sweden, and Norway. The clubs reached critical mass in the '50s and and noted renewed membership through the '80s when they staged growth competitions.

The swinging '60s, as described elsewhere, saw the arrival of an overall facial hair boom that included the moustache, so long as it didn't look military. The fad was so great that the Kent Brushes Company reissued a long-shelved moustache brush for their tending. Stars like Robert Goulet perpetuated the celebrity 'stache as a symbol of sexualized masculinity, later

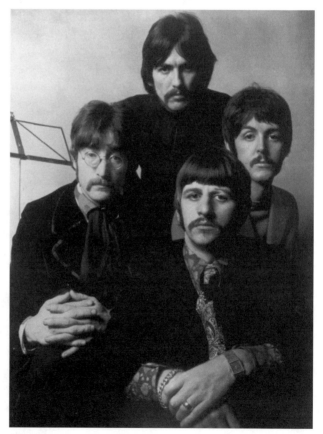

The Beatles.

emulated by actors like Burt Reynolds. The Beatles, ever the trendsetters of the decade, also got into the act; all of them sported moustaches at some point during this period (and occasionally, all at the same time). The Zapata 'stache invoked rebellion, having been named after Emiliano Zapata (1879-1919), a guerrilla during the Mexican revolution of 1917; it was resurrected for several years when Marlon Brando played him in the 1956 film *Viva Zapata!* Later in the decade, the hippie movement saw the flowering of all forms of facial hair, including classic 'staches on stars like Jimi Hendrix.

Jimi Hendrix.

Another classic, the gay moustache, appeared in the 1970s, inspired by the Village People and ultra-macho clones (see Chapter 8). Some believe its evolution into a gay or bisexual signifier explains the ongoing demise of the moustache for straight men in the '80s and '90s. But in all fairness, a lot of smarmy heterosexual swingers with Saturday night fever wore them, too.

Keeping all these historical trends in mind, it is apparent that certain groups have steadfastly eschewed fads and kept growing what they never lost: cops, firemen, construction workers, Greeks, Turks, Indians, Pakistanis, Bulgarians, African Americans, athletes, Southern California rockers, and men with cleft palate repairs are a few faithful examples. (With regard to cops, the Los Angeles Police Department is said to have once deliberated for thirteen weeks to compose rules regulating the wearing of moustaches, concluding that they had to be short, of natural colour, and not worn below the vermilion border of the upper lip or the corners of the mouth.)

In 1967, The Beatles gave away cardboard moustaches with their album *Sgt. Pepper's Lonely Hearts Club Band.*

The '70s, '80s, and even the '90s saw certain celebrities whose moustaches were almost as famous as they were: actor Burt Reynolds, Olympic swimmer Mark Spitz, legal eagle Alan Dershowitz, singer Stevie Wonder, media magnate Ted Turner, film critic Gene Shalit, beach-detective Tom Selleck, and Canadian singer Burton Cummings (lead singer of the Guess Who) are but a few. All have, at one time or another, repackaged themselves without lip-fuzz, perhaps in search of a more youthful look, but most returned to their trademark moustache before too long.

Stevie Wonder.

As I finished composing my clipped 'stache history, I checked out the web to take the millennial pulse on the issue. A fun website I consulted called *www.mustachesummer.com* lists the fifteen sexiest moustaches of all time, in the following order: Sam Elliot (cowboy actor), Tom Selleck, Rollie Fingers (baseball hall-of-famer), Ned Flanders (devout *Simpsons* star), Bea Arthur (who struggled with menopausal growth on *Maude*), Charlie Chaplin, the quintessential "'70s singles bar guy," Gabriel Kaplan (from *Welcome Back, Kotter*), Dirk Dastardly (cartoon villain from *The Wacky Races*), Clark Gable (in *Gone With The Wind*), Colonel Sanders (KFC king), Yosemite Sam (Bugs Bunny nemesis and gold-rusher), the character Jek Porkins from *Star Wars*, and Wilford Brimley (star of those wholesome Quaker Oats television ads). On another website, men share stories from their personal moustache growth experiences, with advice and support readily provided. Yet another misguided web-soul hopes to reclaim the 'stache for "manly heterosexuals." An ongoing popular series of print advertisements promoting milk and reissued on the

Burton Cummings.

web shows celebrities like Naomi Campbell, Britney Spears, and the cast of *Survivor* with milk moustaches. Ironically, these faux 'staches were voted the most popular ones of the '90s, as the real things had all but vanished.

Finally, a 1997 *Wall Street Journal* article spoke of the plight of the modern Turkish man who has long viewed the moustache as a masculine symbol of uncompromising nomad spirit and yet realizes that it clashes with his wish to appear contemporary and competitive (read: clean-shaven) in North American and European cultures. A whole visual, political short-hand is now being lost: once upon a time, left-ists had bushy expressions, rightists had droops to the chin, Sunni Muslims were severely clipped, and Alevi Muslims had curls into the mouth – all abandoned in the name of foreign trade and through increasing exposure to American culprits like CNN and MTV. Even the political die-hards were thinking twice about their upper lips.

Meanwhile, back in the U.S., currently there are some ten million millennial men thought to be wear-ing moustaches. (Those who want to but cannot are now able to undergo micro-transplants or to buy mini-'stache wigs fastened with adhesive.) For those imperfect types among us, the classic 'stache hides bad teeth, lip defects, facial scars, softens a mean mouth, or breaks the line of a long face. For more creative types, it can be waxed, dyed, twirled, and dipped in various sauces prior to kissing. Modern adolescents and college kids across North America who have taken to 'stache-growing contests, appear to favour the Fu Manchu, the pencil-thin, the waxed, and the pointy in combo with grunge, stubble, goatees, and soul patches, but seldom the military-bushy. Fashion watchers repeatedly predict an imminent return of the 'stache. It hasn't quite happened, though they're pop-ping up in print advertisements and on fashion run-ways with some regularity. Rare as moustaches are nowadays, what we see when we look at them depends entirely on our age, generation, ethnicity, and knowl-edge of history.

In 1944, a certain Miss Effron in the *New York Times*

Scientific research, commissioned by the Guinness Brewing Company, found that the average mousta-chioed Guinness drinker traps a pint and a half of the creamy nectar every year. Now that Guinness is UK£ 2.10; a pint, this is the equivalent of an annual moustache tax of UK£ 4.58.

summed things up beautifully: "...the moustache plays many roles today — South American suavity, French affectation, Sicilian villainy. It's Chaplin-pathetic, Hitler-psychopathic, Gable-debonair, Lou Lehr-wacky. It perplexes. It fascinates. It amuses and it repulses."

Though I have no idea who Lou Lehr is, I couldn't agree more.

SIDEBURNS

When you think of sideburns, the image most likely to pop in your head is that of Elvis Presley. He had extra bad 'burns — spectacular growths which fanned out with his advancing age and girth. They made his face seem rebellious, virile, even feral, and induced parental panic about premarital sex and juvenile deliquency (at least those parents who weren't secretly lusting after him themselves). It's safe to say that Elvis is the God of Sideburns — he brought them back from Victorian slumber and made them his personal trademark. Elvis impersonators may fall short in the height, weight, or outfit departments, but they know the importance of his sideys and always manage to get them dead-on. But there is more to sideburn history than The King.

Lest we forget, five American presidents wore exemplary sets: John Q. Adams, Martin Van Buren, Andrew Jackson, John Tyler, and Zachary Taylor. And if you're old enough, perhaps you even sprouted some of your own back in the 1970s (though you have since wisely destroyed all photographic evidence). But don't feel ashamed — as it turns out, for centuries men have arranged wisps of hair from the temple down as part of elaborate coiffures. Sideburns made their first serious appearance during Biblical times when the

Elvis Presley.

Hamathites and Hittites wore dangling, braided versions, but hair worn along the sides of the head had been cultivated as early as 400 BC. It wasn't until the 18th century that sideburns made a huge stylistic impact on both sides of the pond. Called side-whiskers (*favoris* in France), they could be thin and straggly, full and cut, worn above or below the ear, vertical, or veering off at a rather severe right angle.

Sideburns on Prince Edward.
Sir William Beechey, National Archives of Canada C-4297.

Gradually, each variant of sideburns had a name: Picadilly weepers flowed to six inches or more below the chin — Dundrearies, named after Lord Dundreary in Southern's play *Our American Cousin* (the one Lincoln was watching when he was assassinated), were similar but shorter. Mutton chops (lamb chops in the U.S., *cotelettes* in France) looked like you were wearing a meaty dinner on your cheeks. *La Barbe a la Souvaroff* called for a chic trim set of sideys joining an equally thin moustache; though Russian in origin, it was an extremely popular style in the British Army. (Elsewhere, in Eastern Europe, the Jewish sect called the Chassidim was established in 1750 in Poland; its men grew classic ringlets for religious reasons based on their reading of Leviticus.)

Mutton chops on Canadian politician Oliver Mowat. *Archives of Ontario Acc 1750, S-325.*

By 1835, things grew so out of hand (as it were) that the Americans unofficially decided to restrict growth below the earlobe in the name of decency, at least among the military. But back in England, where the growths were called sidebars and sideboards, the look was bushy and formidable. Sir Arthur Sullivan of Gilbert and Sullivan fame (1842-1900) wore a fine set in London at the height of his musical career, as did many a policeman, happy in his lot (or not). American historians remind us that to be precise, the entities known as sideburns are said to be named after U.S. Civil War general Ambrose Burnside, born in Liberty, Indiana in 1824. Although he graduated from West Point in 1847 and commanded the Rhode Island militia at the start of the war, his military career took several turns for the worse due to his own incompetence. Luckily, he ended up a senator until his death in 1875. Burnside still merits an entry in *The Encyclopedia Britannica*, where his remarkable coalescing trademark sideys appear to fill half the page.

Colonel Ambrose Burnside. *Library of Congress, LC-B8172-1625.*

Sideburns, or at least the dangling varieties, fell somewhat out of favour at the end of the 19th century with the advent of the safety razor, but they later exploded back on the scene with the suave, trimmed variety worn beneath plastered-down hair by Rudolf Valentino in the 1920s. Sideburns rapidly shed their avuncular, stodgy, military associations and went studmuffin-matador-gigolo. They certainly enhanced the dark, piercing gaze of Valentino, the bisexual Latin-lover who met an untimely death in 1925. That didn't stop boys in Iowa and North Dakota from imitating his sensuous sideys, ever prompted by the Hollywood dream machine. The next essential icon was born a mere ten years later in Tupelo, Mississippi, and eventually sold 500 million recordings during his life. The aforementioned Elvis (Aron) Presley boldly reinvented the modern sideburn — and his certainly grew in proportion to his plunging necklines, until he died unceremoniously in 1977. Another crooner from the

Canadian Governor General Durham Sydenham, c. 1841. *Archives of Ontario S-155.*

U.K., Engelbert Humperdinck, insists that his own hairy, tight-trousered look predated that of the King. Little matter; sideburns had become a pop extension of the pelvis and oozed sex appeal and teenaged angst and rebellion (if not motorcycle-riding juvenile delinquency) throughout the '50s. In fact, post-war bikers often added sideburns to make them look feral and more frightening – as they terrorized the lunch counters of small-town America.

Sonny Bono.

The psychedelic sixties brought the Mod look which slimmed sideburns down to match pipe pant legs and fitted clothing. Black funksters, greasers, hippies, and bikers prompted by the hit film *Easy Rider* in 1969 all appropriated sideburns as an act of furry freedom and rebellion. So popular was the vertical 'stache that in 1968 Lisa Wigs in the U.S. offered a best-selling fake sideburn kit for the weekend swinger.

During the '70s, if you had platform shoes and a puffy mullet hairdo, you needed big 'burns to balance your act. And you were in good company: Sonny Bono, Isaac Asimov, George Burns, Sean Connery, Clint Eastwood, John Lennon, Joe Namath, William Shatner, and John Wayne were all '70s 'burners. Even Canadian Prime Minister Pierre Trudeau had a fine set, in keeping with the times, as he dated starlets and pirouetted deviously behind the Queen at state functions. By the end of the decade, probably one in three men who frequented discos sported sideburns, a 'stache, or both.

Neil Young.

Sideburns grew more demure in the Reagan-era 1980s. Clean-shaven and corporate was the way to go, at a clipped to well-groomed half-inch at the temple. But the grunge '90s saw the return of all sorts of facial hair in all its glory and the sideburn camp had its definite proponents. The television show *Beverly Hills 90210* had both a good boy (the

Sean Connery as James Bond.

Jason Priestly character) and the bad-boy (played by James Dean lookalike, Luke Perry), both of whom sported very visible sideburns that were soon emulated on high school and university campuses across North America. Hard to know what the statement was — you could be preppy, rich, and screwed up, but still not offend anybody with your facial hair.

At the turn of the millennium, things got considerably more daring — the sideburn could be interrupted, revealing skin-hair stripes or other patterns (fades). The Goth and Dracula-loving set pioneered v-pointy spikes (think Eddy Munster). Club kids made them pencil thin — frond-like, multi-stranded, Chassidic-curly, or Trekkie-sharp. In the film *X-Men*, Hugh Jackman portrayed the mutant Wolverine with a set of major lamb chops, leaving no doubt that sideburns can be unpredictably werewolfish and dangerous as well as sexy. Bikers and gay leathermen of all stripes continued to flirt with sexual-outlaw 'burns to complement their leather-bound look. And World Wrestling Federation stars like The Rock and pro-football players like Dustin Hermanson of the St. Louis Cardinals sported respectable sidewear in noticeable numbers, leading impressionable fans to follow suit.

There is also a new trimming gadget called Prolook for men heeding the call of the sideburn. It consists of a trimming template on an eyeglass-like frame which allows one to choose one of five growth levels and several angles for clipping. But companies like Remington and Schick would not be outdone — all models of electric razors now have sideburn flip-up trimmers, and a number of more generic hair clippers advertise special features for sideburns. You can now be bushy, clipped, long, short, angular, rounded, or asymmetric as you enter sidey heaven.

World's Longest Moustache: According to the *Guinness Book of World Records*, in July 1993, Kalyan Ramji Sain of Sundargarth, India had a moustache that measured 133.4 inches long. (The right side was 67.7 inches long and the left side 65.7 inches long.)

STUBBLE

Stubble, alias the five o'clock shadow or shadow beard, has been around since cavemen first plucked or scraped their faces and for whatever reason, stopped. Until the middle of the 20th century, stubble has had a decidedly negative rep. Photos from the Great Depression show weary, unshaven men in soup kitchens or on the dole line. Ever since, a man sporting such growth is often characterized as lazy, crazy, or down-and-out, the only reasons he could have had to stop shaving. Further, such a man obviously disrespects his female companion, who must wince at his abrasive embrace. This was a look cultivated by pirates, convicts, and crass frat-boys on weekend binges, so any man who sheepishly decided to grow a proper beard thought it best to hide away for the amount of time it took to grow in and look respectable. (In the 1930s Gem Razors coined the phrase "five o'clock shadow" to encourage men to shave a second time each day, as it took mere hours, not days, for stubble to be detected and thus ruin one's credibility.) Unless he was in mourning, a fellow who appeared with stubble in public would invariably be asked if he were ill, when he planned to tidy up, or why he had taken the rather unfortunate decision to grow a beard. After all, everybody remembers that it was stubble, not to mention the shifty eyes and bad suit, that led to Richard Nixon's undoing in the 1960 televised presidential debate with John F. Kennedy. How could you vote for a guy who hadn't bothered to shave before appearing on television?

Granted, Hollywood has offered up a few stubble pioneers as rugged icons, the first being Humphrey Bogart. He looked extra-tough, if unruly, as he bantered endlessly with Katharine Hepburn on *The African Queen*. Fans agreed that Bogey was okay, that you might imitate his look on a weekend fishing trip, but never at the office. Twenty years later, Clint Eastwood and a batch of spaghetti western stars looked rugged on the wild frontier, but your wife (or mother) would never stand for the outlaw look at home. They would remind you that cowboys didn't have access to running water and then ask for your excuse.

Only in the 1980s did the shadow become chic when sported by Don Johnson and his cronies on the television series *Miami Vice*. The look was suddenly christened "designer stubble," as it soon popped up in advertisements and on the fashion runways along with deconstructed pastel-coloured jackets and shoes without socks. Stubble was said to sharpen a man's features, offsetting cheekbones and jawlines, and it probably did for those who were already blessed in the bone department. Stubble supposedly announced that a man was fiercely independent, and no slave to the razor or an uptight boss. He may have just gotten up, but he was ready for a corporate takeover or drug bust. (Little did the uninitiated realize that the style required very close clipping and daily maintenance to appear so cutting edge.) Women said the look was a turn-on, even if it resulted in unintentional dermabrasion during kissing or other forms of intimacy.

By the end of the decade, stubble was out — clean lines in clothing were back, which called for clean faces as well. That's not to say that shadow beards have not appeared with some regularity on famous faces over the last fifteen years. George Michael, the Baldwin brothers, Bob Geldof, John Travolta, Kevin Spacey, Edgar Bronfman Jr., professional athletes on hiatus (or post-hangover), and heartthrobs like Ricky Martin have all gone for stubble when it suited them. Nowadays, every single fashion magazine features models with a day or two's growth, but the look is less calculated and manicured, and is often worn accompanied by other *accoutrements* like sideburns. After all, modern guys feel that *Miami Vice* fuzz was a tad precious. And nobody wants to resemble his dad on holiday, a spaghetti cowboy, or a middle-aged detective. Better to look like you just rolled out of bed.

The owner of the Oakland A's baseball team paid each of his players $300 to grow a 'stache in 1971.

THE GOATEE

Goatees swept North America and Europe in the mid- to late 1990s, and this phenom facial hair style has continued unabated into the new millennium — much to the chagrin of my hairdresser, Lucy, who hates them. What is currently referred to as the goatee, however, is something of a catch-all category. It encompasses any partial or chin beard as opposed to the full enchilada, which would otherwise include a moustache, chin whiskers, and sideburns all coalescing into one. Technically, the true goatee denotes a small tuft of hair dangling from the chin, with or without a moustache; its name comes from what the billygoat grows spontaneously. Its greatest aesthetic benefit has always been to hide a weak or pointy chin and to allow adolescent boys to believe that they wouldn't be carded in bars if they grew one.

The devil in a 20th-century advertisement.

John Sulak, in a cheeky *Requestline.com* article, reminds us that historically, the most famous and iconographic goatee is that worn by Satan. There has been a long association between the devil, goats, cloven hooves, horniness, and bestiality. The devil/goat connection no doubt derives from the legend of Pan, the bearded half-man, half-goat god who became vilified by Christians because of his love for music, nature, and sexual debauchery. Satan's beard is invariably portrayed as pointed, dark, and sinister, and indicates the way to hell in its direction of growth. Lest we forget, the partial chin beard has also been worn by more reputable types, including Egypt's King Tutankhamen, who wore a square-shaped version. (The Egyptians were known to wear both real and fake goatees.) The ancient Moabites of biblical times shaved off their sideburns, leaving only a chin beard. Christian IV, King of Denmark (1577-1648), was a dapper dude

King Tutankhamen.

Satan, in "The Temptation of Christ" by Juan de Flandes. *By Juan de Flandes (from Queen Isabella's private chapel), NGA.*

with his chin beard, a hair braid, and single earring, a look that would not be out of place today.

Things progressed merrily when a forked-beard variant emerged between approximately 1350 and 1400 throughout Europe. William Shakespeare makes references to over ninety beards in his various plays, but himself wore a small goatee and moustache. The goatee achieved its greatest credibility under the tutelage of Sir Anthony Van Dyck, a Flemish painter to the court of Charles I (1599-1641). He sported a trademark beard which was thereafter referred to as the Vandyke, and also painted a series of portraits of men wearing his own style of beard. One wonders if having a Vandyke was a prerequisite for being painted by the great portraitist. The 16th and 17th centuries saw the rapid growth of chin-beard variants including the bodkin, stiletto, and hammer cut in Spain, England, and France, who were in perpetual competition with one another to come up with new styles.

One style, a narrower, longer version called the Imperial, re-emerged when it was worn with distinction by Napoleon III (1852-78). Ludwig II (1845-1886), the King of Bavaria, and Victor Emmanuel (1820-78), the first King of Italy, both wore fine goatees. The style had already "jumped the pond" and was not atypical in the U.S. in the 19th century. Columnist Edith Sessions Tupper condemned the goatee in her column in the *Chicago Chronicle*, stating her

William Shakespeare.

preference for a clean-shaven man, as a Vandyke or goatee usually signified "a man ... who was selfish, sinister, and pompous as a peacock." Ironically, in the 1850s it became an iconic symbol of the U.S. federal government as worn by the omnipresent Uncle Sam. Soldiers on both sides of the Civil War wore goatees as a badge of honour and rugged defiance. General George Custer had one at his Last Stand, as did Confederate General Robert Toombs (1810-55). Buffalo Bill perfected his cowboy act touring the U.S. with his distinctive long-haired look. In late 19th-century Paris, in the *Quartier Latin*, intellectuals, poets, bohemians, and musicians sipped coffee and stroked their chin tufts while deep in thought. Physicians throughout Europe also looked to the

Buffalo Bill. *Moffett, Library of Congress, LC-USZ62-2050.*

style to appear more scholarly and authoritative. In 1900, Sigmund Freud published his *Interpretation of Dreams* sporting one of the most famous partial beards in history. Ever since, every stage caricature of a shrink requires a German-accented actor with a salt and pepper goatee. The Russian Revolution in 1917 was led by the goateed Vladimir Ilyich Lenin (1870-1924), whose communist cronies also favoured facial hair. It's here that the chin beard sprouted persistent lefty associations, which is probably why so few western politicians sport them today.

Although beards were largely eradicated by allied

North American soldiers during World War II, a beatnik look sprouted in jazz clubs throughout the U.S. soon after the war's end. The look was said to have been created by Dizzy Gillespie, the clown prince of jazz, who wore a goatee, iron-rimmed shades, and a beret. When asked about his goatee by *Downbeat Magazine* in 1989, the trumpet player explained that his goatee was "strictly utilitarian, man! ... Nothing fetish about it. First, it gives my lips strength. You know what hair did for Samson. It's protection, too. Can't afford to let a razor get too loose too close to those chops." Gillespie's contemporary, Charlie "Bird" Parker, was a goateed be-bop sax player and heroin junkie whose bearded look became linked to the dark edge of drug culture. Fortunately, the squeaky-clean pop conductor Mitch Miller and influential author John Steinbeck had more reassuring goatees in the 1950s. By 1955 *Look* magazine identified the

1929 poster commemorating Lenin's death.

Van Dyck, now re-spelled "Vandyke," as the most popular beard style in America.

By the 1960s, some very prominent Americans sported the goatee. Folk singer Burl Ives had a smash hit with "I Know an Old Lady," and his greying goatee suggested a look of both distinction and grandfatherly familiarity. Black political leader Malcolm X wore a goatee, which made him look intense, studious, and credible. Colonel Sanders, who had been a jack of all trades (including a lawyer) before franchising his recipe for fried chicken with its eleven secret herbs and spices, wore a very Southern goatee complete with bow tie and white suit, making him a fast food icon. The howling gravel-voiced Wolfman Jack, a popular

Burl Ives. *Carl Van Vechten. LC Lot 12735, no. 567.*

'60s disc jockey who later moved into television, wore a goatee with longish hair appropriate to his nickname.

The website *Goatee.com* suggests that the goatee may have been done irreparable damage when Americans watched the enormously popular television show *Dobie Gillis* between 1959 and 1963. The comedy featured a character named Maynard Krebs (played by Bob Denver, of *Gilligan's Island* fame); Krebs was a gentle, goateed vagabond, but appeared to be something of a loser. While prominent Europeans like British prime minister Benjamin Disraeli and conductor Sir Thomas Beecham wore more distinguished goatees, Americans apparently came to link the style to Krebs, and an emerging symbol of a ne'er-do-well lost generation. Speaking of television, the current batch of generation XYZ goatee wearers are no doubt more influenced by the cartoon *Scooby Doo, Where Are You?*, whose goofy co-star Shaggy sported a straggly goatee.

Colonel Sanders.

Wolfman Jack.

The early 1990s saw the emergence of the musical phenomenon known as grunge, as typified by the Seattle band Nirvana; its ill-fated lead singer, Kurt Cobain, sang of alienation and disconnection, with blond and sometimes darker scruff on his chin. A whole generation of youth, both in Europe and America, listened to the likes of Nirvana and Pearl Jam, among others; their facial hair expressed disenfranchisement in ways meant to be both bohemian and masculine.

Bob Denver as
Maynard Krebs.

Throughout the late '80s and early '90s, other musicians, actors, and athletes experimented with the goatee. Prince and George Michael pioneered clipped, precisely styled ones. Brat-packers Robert Downey Jr., Charlie Sheen, and Johnny Depp grew facial hair in order to cultivate a macho, bad-boy look. In 1994, baby-faced Tom Cruise and Brad Pitt grew chin tufts to rough things up. Anthony Edwards of *E.R.* fame and Greg Vaughan of the Cincinnati Reds were also prominent goatee wearers in the '90s. Even Paul Reubens (a.k.a. PeeWee Herman) butched up his

Kurt Cobain.

George Michael.

look with a 'tee. Fred Durst of the band Limp Bizkit pioneered the popular look known as the chin strip (though 19th-century journalist William E. Hashell wore one for most of his career); this style requires a precise line down the centre of the chin as opposed to the dangling goatee. In the late '90s, Jeff Boswell wore a modern version of the King Tut. Spike Lee, director of *Malcolm X* and *Do the Right Thing*, continues to wear a goatee, as does baseball star Mark McGwire, who broke the home run record for a single season in 1998. World Wrestling Federation's 1996 king of the ring, Stone Cold Steve Austin, periodically sports a tuft goatee.

What's intriguing about the neo-goatee is how it has been adopted by radically opposite segments of male society. As discussed in Chapter 8, gay men adopted the goatee as their own to make them look more severe, masculine, and buff. The connection between facial hair and masculinity that escalates into neo-Nazism and fascism was driven home by actor Edward Norton in the chilling 1998 film *American History X*. Klingons on *Star Trek: The Next Generation* and other spinoffs sported a futuristic version of the Imperial, also known as the Royal. A plague of boy bands carved out an endless variety of goatee variants, to make them appear more masculine, streetwise, or musically serious; Joey Fatone of 'N Sync and Kevin Richardson and A.J. McLean of the Backstreet Boys took precision shaving into the next millennium. Circle beards (or beavers, because of their resemblance to female genitalia), did just that —

Brad Pitt.

Fred Durst.

Edward Norton.

A.J. McLean.

circled the mouth in men who perhaps were ambivalent about their sexuality. Soul patches (or "flavour-savers"), made popular by singers like Frank Zappa and Tom Waits, punctuated the chin as circles, squares, rectangles, or diamonds, sometimes dyed bright colours. Today, you can find goatees almost everywhere, from the corporate boardroom to the campus classroom.

Throughout history, the goatee and its variants have moved from diabolical to imperial to military to cool to tough to neo-Nazi to athletic to intergalactical to corporate/academic. It has thrived on the chins of latecomers desperate for distinction. Ironically, the goatee may have become the equivalent of the middle-age ponytail, once lambasted in Douglas Coupland's *Generation X* as a universal symbol of conformist

Frank Zappa.

Tom Waits.

rebellion. Fortunately, twenty-somethings are re-inventing it as we speak with fades, piercings, threading, dyes, braiding, and unpredictable directions of growth.

❧ *Chapter 11* ❧

THE 20TH
CENTURY BEARD

W hat did the beard mean as it fanned into the 20th century? If we scratch our chins and pause for review, it had already been the badge of kings (or slaves), saintly (or perfidious), a symbol of devout believers (or infidels), a sign of robust health (or a bacteria trap), wise and fatherly (or cold and war-mongering), virile (or a foppish affectation), beloved by women (or a cause for divorce), the pride of the British Empire (or the barbaric mark of foreigners), taxed if grown (or not grown properly), and a young man's embellishment (or an old man's crumb-filled shame). The conventional, predictable beard was about to change forever.

Things would certainly get much more interesting as the century progressed, but not right away. This delay was in large part due to the success of Gillette's safety razor, which facilitated home-shaving and contributed to an ever-growing pressure for modern, industrialized Americans to be "clean-shaven" (hairy obviously suggesting dirty, old-country ways). There was also an increasing ambivalence towards facial hair because of the historical and cultural baggage associated with it. Beards, in fact, practically disappeared from world view from 1900 to 1950, except on the faces of a few "old-timers" and eccentrics. Western clergymen were generally clean-shaven, as were most politicians and members of the royal houses of Europe. If worn at all, hybrid beard styles like the Olympus, the miner, and square or forked shapes had supplanted some of the old standards. In the U.S., the moustache hung on for the first twenty years of the new century, mostly of the classic handlebar and kaiser varieties. (The latter, named after the German kaiser, was so popular that it spawned an industry of kaiser moustache trainers, to keep the ends pointing perkily upwards.)

Back at the beginning of the century, a moralistic attitude toward facial hair started to creep in, suggesting that bearded men were sinister (like Rasputin) or had something to hide ("behind hedges lie wrong

In a 1999 annual survey of women's opinions on male hair conducted by Just for Men, a hair-dye company, 61 percent of Baby Boomers (age 35-44) found a moustache to be a turn on, 25 percent found beards sexy, and 33 percent of Generation Xers (age 25-34) "swooned over goatees."

thoughts"). A growing hygiene movement condemned facial hair as a breeding ground for nasty bacteria; in 1903, the *Chicago Chronicle* reported that the average beard harboured up to 200,000 "misanthropic microbes." In 1907 *Harper's* magazine reported on a proposed bill by a New Jersey legislator who thought it wise to tax filthy whiskers in the U.S., as had been done previously in Russia. Soldiers in World War I dispensed with the beard but continued to sprout various forms of military moustaches which often suggested rank.

In the 1920s, comedians Charlie Chaplin, with his short brush moustache, and Chester Conklin, with his fake walrus, became huge film stars. They were the first to use a furry trademark to render themselves unforgettable to their fans. Both were imitated widely, but surely not for anything remotely related to sex appeal. During this period, men wore their hair short and parted in the middle and generally abandoned lip fuzz until occasionally prompted by the new royalty — sexy Hollywood actors like Douglas Fairbanks, Robert Taylor, and Ronald Colman. Overall, red-blooded Americans remained somewhat ambivalent about the 'stache because it still sig-

Charlie Chaplin.

nified the cad, fop, or foreigner. As 20th-century clergy and kings were no longer the arbiters of decorum or trendsetting, Hollywood happily took over the role and has shamelessly exploited it ever since. Thanks to them, plastered-down hair and permanents called Marcel waves became popular around 1922. For a time, a hot sideburn craze swept under the inspiration of megastar Rudolf Valentino. The message was clear: if facial hair was present on a serious actor's face, it probably had something to do with sex.

By the end of the 1920s, beards were all but

A handsome man is handsomer with the proper style of beard, and homely or coarse features are softened by the searing of some becoming whiskers, which detract from the coarseness of the features. A full beard when properly trimmed, becomes most every man, but when it does not grow full enough, or of any even thickness, it may be shaven in various styles. The short, broad face is improved by a chin beard, while a long, thin

banished, so much so that a *New Statesmen* article in 1935 concluded that "bearded men enjoyed all of the privileges of bearded women." Within a matter of years, a man in Western society would rather die than resemble Lenin and Stalin (or Marx for that matter), as facial hair had acquired yet another new but entirely enduring 20th-century meaning — that of dictator, communist, or revolutionary (see Chapter 2). The beard has been the kiss of death for Western politicians ever since. American and Canadian GIs were clean-shaven in World War II, while their British RAF counterparts sported handlebars. (One of the reasons beards were banned in the forces during World War II was that a soldier who found himself in water after a crash might collect thick diesel oil on his whiskers, leading to suffocation.) Not surprisingly, the kaiser and Hitleresque brush styles vanished altogether by 1945. Because of its genocidal implications, the latter remains one of the few facial hair taboos.

By the war's end, the New York Post suggested that conservative (i.e., non-Germanic) moustaches lent

Fredrich Nietzsche.

an air of confidence, dignity, distinction, and maturity to the male face. Before long, the prosperous post-war period saw facial hair sprout anew, often as an act of rebellion against conformity, militarism, or even suburban boredom. Beatniks, bohemians, artists, and poets all sprouted intello-tufts of disenfranchisement in Europe and in North America. A new emphasis on individual style melded with fashion tribalism took hold, and facial hair frequently played a role in these emerging looks. Initially, the majority of American men during this time embraced brushcuts, flat-tops, and a clean-shaven, collegiate look. But by 1954, *Barber's Journal* reported spotting an ever-increasing number of beards on Madison Avenue, at New York City colleges, and in bohemian centres like Greenwich Village. In fact, a '50s guy now had a number of fashion tribes to choose from (all of which still exist in some form in the new millennium). Beats (disparagingly called beatniks), under the tutelage of clean-shaven bards Jack Kerouac and Neal Cassady, professed to be indifferent to style but embraced the goatee and black clothing as the essential anti-establishment uniform. Folkies in their bright homespun colours were hippie precursors who yearned for the simplicity of country life while playing acoustic guitars; sprouting a beard was a significant part of being a "natural man." West-coast surfers wore loose, striped, casual clothes and sandals when not riding big waves — and made the blond beard cool, instead of feeble and faded. And when Earth-shattering Elvis came onto the scene, white hipster lookalikes quickly sprouted slick pompadours and major sideburns in honour of their king. Suddenly there were so many ways to be furry and unconventional!

The ubiquity of mass media, in film, television, or print, guaranteed rapid propagation of clothing fads and facial hairstyles worldwide in ways never possible before. What was different was that men were sprouting facial hair as an expression of individualism and creativity, rather than out of unquestioning allegiance to an authoritarian religious, political, or socioeconomic group. Allegiance belonged to these new cool tribes, who cultivated distinct looks but shared a discontent with urban, middle-class life.

The fuzzy 1960s were celebrated in the hit musical *Hair*, which more than captured prevailing psychedelic attitudes — free fuzz, free-flowing duds, free love, and definite inhaling. Hair was by now undeniably sexual, and there was no shame in letting it all hang out; the longer the better, on both men and women. There were vociferous objections from the churches and politicians regarding this libidinous, wild aspect of physical appearance and what they considered a dangerous blending of genders. But for the first time in history, their "authority machine" complaints fell

face is broadened and appears shorter by wearing side whiskers. A moustache shades off a large nose, also covers a homely mouth, bad teeth, and thick lips. The Imperial (or goatee) is trying to certain types of faces, although it has been extensively worn and is still used by many.

A moustache should always be dressed or rolled to give it a natural, easy appearance. When it is rolled on paper or curled with an iron or slate pencil, it should be combed out in an easy and natural way. Artificial appearance should always be avoided. It is very poor taste to leave the moustache rolled up in a bunch.

– E.M. Robinson, styling tips from *The Art of Barbering* (1906)

Bearded man as central promotional image for Burt's Bees product. *Courtesy of Burt's Bees, Inc.*

on deaf ears. Hair was where it was at, although the peace-love mantra for all things hirsute did preclude the wearing of moustaches for a time, because of their associations with militaristic pursuits. Indeed, the wearing of all various forms of facial hair increasingly signified discontent over the Vietnam War which raged on during this period. Long hair, lamb chops, and beards, together with love beads and ethnic garb, became the uniform of the conscientious objector and draft dodger.

Meanwhile, the more "respectable" '60s male disavowed flower power and embraced a batch of new and improved electric shavers and aerosol foams. He consulted fashion-conscious "hairstylists" who had stealthily replaced the now old-fashioned barbers, seemingly overnight.

Throughout the 1970s, hair was big (i.e., voluminous), "styled" (not long and unruly), and sometimes permed and blow-dried to within an inch of its life. Elvis continued wearing his trademark sideburns and Burt Reynolds his moustache, but by the end of the decade the prevailing look was either scrubbed-face preppy or disco-smarmy. In the U.S., the moustache worn by gay clones and rock stars including Freddie Mercury became a definite signifier of gay, bi, or swinger orientation, but like a lot of gay fads, promptly spilled into the mainstream. By 1977, skinheads and punks in the U.K. were getting buzz-shaved and pierced, but short of clipped sideburns, facial hair was not a part of the look.

Freddie Mercury.

The 1980s were largely a down time for facial hair, as people gradually recovered from disco and hairspray toxicity and got down to serious business. A few prominent people persisted with trademark styles — Billy Dee Williams, Tom Selleck, and Geraldo Rivera kept their moustaches for their roles as television celebrities. The reinvented five o'clock shadow, popularized by television's *Miami Vice*, was said to lend a chiseled, tough look and to hide multiple chins (which in fact it did not). Mr T., the black action star of *The A-Team*, pioneered precision trimming of his beard (and hair), leading black kids to shave fades on their scalps. (In twenty years' time, they would be doing this to their beards as well.) Lest we forget, the '80s also saw the emergence of several new fashion tribes who were busy working on new looks and new musical sounds. B-boys wore moustaches and sportswear, while in Seattle, a "grunge" look was taking hold, consisting of limp hair, scruffy goatees, and loose-fitting clothing. Meanwhile, middle-aged boomers sprouted rather desperate pony-tails and had an ear or two pierced.

Soon after, all grew chillingly quiet on the facial hair front across the world. In 1987, headlines reported that even Syria was declaring a war on beards because of their links to Muslim fundamentalism, one more indication that they were seen as marginal.

The impact of African Americans on facial hair

Marvin Gaye.

Martin Luther King. *Yoichi Okamoto/LBJ Library.*

styles certainly deserves its own commentary. Lloyd Boston, in his illustrated book *Men of Color: Fashion, History, Fundamentals*, argues that popular black styles — whether rapper, preppie, gentrified, dapper, tough, gangsta, jock, Rasta, or New Islam, were all about cultural survival and celebrating difference from the aesthetic forged by a powerful (mostly clean-shaven) white majority. Fashion also allowed affiliations to be identified whether to a type of music, a sport, or a political, university or neighbourhood group. Facial hair styles have remained an enduring form of expression for black men regardless of whatever fad had taken hold around them. Moustaches have always been a constant on prominent faces: Duke Ellington, Louis Armstrong, Muddy Waters, Cab Calloway, Miles Davis, Count Bassie, Langston Hughes, Marvin Gaye, Jimi Hendrix, Martin Luther King, Jesse Jackson, Sammy Davis Jr., Quincy Jones, Marvin Gaye, Isaac

Hayes, George Benson, Wynton Marsalis, Jim Brown, Jimmie (J.J.) Walker, Arsenio Hall, Eddie Murphy, Evander Holyfield, and Don King are a few examples. Beards grew free and full under the political influences of Pan-Africanism, Black Power, Rastafari, and new Islam. The modern goatee was for all intents and purposes re-invented by Dizzy Gillespie. No better sideburns existed than on the face of Clarence William III as Link on television's *The Mod Squad*. The Blaxploitation films of the seventies saw Richard Roundtree sport the first *Shaft* look ('stache and 'burns), while Ron O'Neal had a funky, mean 'stache in *Superfly*. As we forge ahead into the new millennium, many black pop stars, hip-hop artists, and rappers have upped the facial hair ante. As Boston stresses in his book, there's no doubt that trendwatchers will continue to look to the clothing, hair, and beard styles of the black community for years to come.

Jesse Jackson. *Warren K. Leffler, Library of Congress, LC-U9-41583.*

❧ *Chapter 12* ❧

THE
POSTMODERN BEARD

S o what really happened in the 1990s? Why did I and most of my friends jump on the facial hair bandwagon, adopting all manners of style? Paradoxically, what marked the start of the greatest boom in facial hair since Victorian times actually consisted of two quiet exits: that of designer stubble (short of a few weekend hangover stragglers) and the once ubiquitous swinger moustache.

In yet another reversal, the new hairless era was ironically heralded with proclamations in 1993 that facial hair was now prohibited in seventeen U.S. state police forces. However, by the mid-1990s, the first real facial hair craze since '60s sideburns and the '70s 'stache took hold and even now shows no apparent signs of slowing down. The mini-beard was back.

It began with the goatee and its variants, which had been worn by grunge musicians like Kurt Cobain. In no time at all, it spread to all quarters and across all age groups: club and rave kids who braided it and painted it red or green; dot-com millionaires seeking to look less nerdish; middle-aged professionals toning down their conservatism; rock stars like Rob Zombie reconfiguring the unruly "wild man" look, complete with shock makeup; neo-lefties, fascist punks, and young next-big-thing actors started trying to look older and tougher; post-punk Brit head-shavers and legions of gay guys came to resemble each other whether they liked it or not. Athletes and musicians, ever in the public eye, probably did the most to propagate the look, but nobody deserves full credit as the style spread like wildfire throughout Europe and North America, so much so that Penelope Green in *Men's Fashion of the Times* bitterly "bemoaned" the return of facial hair in 2000. She cited *GQ* writer Owen Edwards, who spoke of "a plague of goatees," "failed facial experiments," and

Rob Zombie.

cowardly equivalents of "impermanent tattoos" in an era of pointless piercings and mindless skin-painting. For some reason, Green particularly despised another huge '90s facial hair variant, the small tuft below the chin called the soul patch, jazz, switch, or flavour-saver. Once called a "mouche" (i. e., "housefly"), the soul patch now comes in various shapes including circles, squares, triangles, rectangles, diamonds, and line-skids down to the chin. It has been spotted on actors like Keanu Reeves, Eric Stoltz, and Josh Brolin, and athletes like Arizona Diamondbacks pitcher Randy Johnson. A popular style overlooked by our angry columnist is the circle beard, a continuous moustache-goatee combo circling the mouth (not unlike an unjoined moustache-chin beard combo reminiscent of the old Imperiale). Throughout the '90s, polymorphous twenty-somethings and club-kids were the most creative in combining hairy patches to hugely original effect. They reinvented bushy sideburns, the Lincoln beard, secular Hassidic curls, the teenaged fuzz-'stache and other straggles, looks that eventually reached the fashion runways of Paris and Milan.

Another hot *fin de siècle* trend which seems to have no antecedents in history is the snail-trail or pencil-beard. This style consists of pencil-thin, architecturally precise lines for sideburns, with an accompanying face-frame or box-beard. It's a difficult look to maintain; most men have their hairdressers carve it out first and then maintain it with triple-blade razors and purloined black eyebrow pencils. The look has been pioneered by gay men, hip-hop artists, and boy-band stars like A.J. McLean. It can look extremely severe, making a pointy face even more angular. David Graham, a fashion reporter for the *Toronto Star*, warns that "No matter what people think or hope, it simply won't lend structure to a weak face." Nonetheless, it seems to provide an endless variety of lines on young faces in downtowns across North America and Europe.

But back to the burning question that had me drop my razor and pick up my plume: why does facial hair continue to fascinate us, even as we rage on into the new millennium? Multiple theories abound. We've already looked at evolution, sex, and aggression in Chapter 7. I wisely decided to ask a woman for her take; Barbara Alexander, a Toronto fashion trend predictor, movie make-up artist, and CEO of Paintbox Industries, sees facial hair as a reaction to feminism:

> Androgyny is out. Men want to look tough and virile again. Men can grow hair and most women can't so a beard can express that. Men also have the option, unlike women, of completely changing their look or hiding flaws like a weak chin for free, without going under the knife.

Barbara added that guys still tend to over-estimate the appeal of face fuzz for women, many of whom do not find it pleasing to the eye or to the touch. Is fur an unconscious macho backlash, or hopeless self-sabotage in the dating department?

Men I spoke to said they like to play with a rebellious side, invoking many of the negative historical connotations of facial hair — the horny goat, devil, villain, commie, aesthete, subversive, bohemian — while at the same time maintaining respectable, even high-paying jobs. It's also not a permanent decision; a guy has the option to shave if his experiment draws fire from a boss or partner. There are many hairy psychological archetypes discussed earlier that men toy with consciously or unconsciously, and not infrequently subvert. A youthful vegetarian student might, for example, choose a Colonel Sanders look. A trucker might grow a long-upturning moustache without knowing or caring who Mephisphales or Dali were. A Jesuit novice I know currently looks like Lenin but without the socialist idealism. A guy might cultivate a benevolent Santa Claus or Moses look and surprise

Mephistopheles. *Engraving by Lammel from the original by Pecht (c. 1860).*

people with his competitiveness or surliness. Most men I surveyed are completely oblivious to the histories of the styles they wear, although there's very little new under the sun or on the chin. In the West, they make their decisions free of religious or political interference, but try to get away with what they can in the corporate world.

Moses.

Regrettably, there are now simply too many "late-adapters," as David Graham calls them — what was once an act of individuality or nerve is now a ubiquitous fashion statement: "Once your dentist has a goatee, it's time to change your look." There is also the issue of the media. Advertising would have us believe that although a man may be successful and possess all the material trappings, he is in actual fact a rebel at heart, and no one's corporate slave. And by driving Car X or sprouting Facial Hairstyle Y, he can show the world just how free he is. As it was for an ancient Roman, the new man's beard is a visible sign of liberty and independent status. And maybe eternal youth: a soul patch or chin-curtain might make a middle-aged man look hotter, badder, younger, or meaner. It might also make him nothing more than a bogus bohemian with a bank account. For kids, facial hair continues to be about sex, youth, and rebellion. Alas, for us men over forty, we hope that it is.

And now that we've entered the new millennium, what's next? Jacques Fontaine, a hairdresser who works near Montreal, made a few predictions:

> *Tout va* — anything goes. Ethnic is hot — dreadlocks, Afros - and watch for the return of the mini-mohawk. For facial hair, it's definitely the moustache. I've heard of kids staging moustache-growing contests. You'll see them with hairy chests, just like in the '70s. Also more sideburns than beards. Dyeing hair wild colours will be big, now that there are so many over the counter beard dyes. That

pencil look will continue, but tell your readers to get their stylist to do the blueprint. I've seen some disasters out there. Teen fuzz-patches are on all the runways, like they've just rolled out of bed. I tell you — anything could happen — even long beards. We've not seen the last of facial hair!

As I continued my obsessive face-watching on the streets of Toronto, I couldn't help notice that goatees are still popular, but these days men are colouring them, weaving beads into them, twisting them (to resemble the old screw beard), waxing them to multiple points, and braiding or separating layers with elastic bands. Long, scraggly variants with moustaches (like the Oriental scholar and the King Tut) are back. Growth on the sides of the chin instead of a point are also a common style.

Soul patches are being carved into unusual shapes and dyed fluorescent colours, particularly gold. I've even seen the below-the-chin central skidmark extending defiantly down to the chest or even the navel. Sideburns of all stripes are big again with twenty-something kids, from Dundrearies to lamb chops. Those tricky carved pencil lines are combined with moustaches and fuller goatees, or precisely circle the mouth. Cheek-fades with various patterns are accompanied by face/tongue jewelry or interrupted eyebrows. (Among urban primitives, facial tattooing to resemble hair or incorporating aboriginal designs is popular on the west coast, and cluster piercings to resemble facial hair is big on the east coast.)

Make-up emulating facial hair has also emerged — Lori Jean Swanson of the Cloutier agency in L.A. was quoted in *Men's Fashion of the Times* about applying stipple-sponged stubble, sideburns, and goatees on celebrities. Like the beard-toupés of the '60s, this is ideal for the weekend swinger. As Jacques Fontaine mentioned, the moustache has been threatening to make a comeback for some time, some thirty years after the last real 'stache boom. Recently, I've spotted the Zapata, Fu Manchu, and horseshoe on urban streets.

As I listed all of these looks, transient as some may be, it suddenly occurred to me that with approximately fifteen contemporary moustache variants, five sideburn lengths, and over forty beard styles, combinations and permutations in the new millennium are endless on strictly mathematical grounds. Not all have yet been named, though I'm sure most are being expressed.

Once upon a time, we thought we knew what a beard meant because kings, saints, and philosophers wore them, but now, in the new culture, any familiar symbol can be called into question. When you look at a postmodern bearded face, what you see is a series of projections travelling in both directions, based on age, culture, gender, knowledge of history, professional status, exposure to media icons, and resulting levels of beardophobia (or pogonophilia). As we've seen, because of the beard's rather convoluted history, notions of eros and thanatos, east and west, good and evil, youth and decrepitude, and masculinity and femininity are woven into each strand on one's furry face. In the new millennium, we're destined to remain somewhat perplexed by the meanings of facial hair, and in my opinion, this has allowed it to flourish in styles never seen before. For every man, its growth represents both an inevitability and a choice, an expression of permanence or an accompaniment through transition. Whatever tribe he belongs to, a man's face is his canvas. As long as he has testosterone coursing through his veins, he can choose to reinvent himself.

In whom the fiery Muse revered
The Symbol of a snow-white beard,
Bedewed with meditative tears
Dropped from the lenient cloud of years.

— William Wordsworth, written in a blank leaf of Macpherson's *Ossian*

❧ *Chapter 13* ❧

THE PERSONAL BEARD: GROOMING STRATEGIES

Dear Readers,

Having tantalized you with details and images of historical and modern facial hair styles, I wouldn't be surprised if you wanted to try one yourself. Here are some instructions on growing, tending, trimming and removing your own facial hair variations.

Mr. Block the Barber

PLANNING A BEARD

1) Before beginning to grow your beard, it is advisable to select a style to which you can aspire. This will serve as a measure when determining how long to grow before trimming, and as a guide when it is time to begin grooming your new beard.

2) Examine beards on those around you and in magazines. Once you have selected a basic style, this can be tailored to suit your face and pattern of beard growth.

3) Many CD-ROM makeover kits feature beard and moustache options. Using a digital image of your face, you can apply ready-made facial hair styles, or create your own using a freehand drawing device. You can also order false facial hair to try styles in advance.

4) The same effect can be achieved using photo booth pictures and acetate overlays. You will require two front views, one smiling and one serious, and a left and right profile. Acetate sheets and china markers for drawing your beard can be obtained at an art supply shop. Place the acetate over your photographs, then draw on various styles. Once you select a single style, transfer this directly to the photographs, which you will use as a guide during the initial trimming and shaping.

5) Avoid shaving entirely for the first four to six weeks. This will allow your beard to grow in naturally, and will give you a sense of its colour, pattern, and rate of growth, and will eliminate the risk of over-trimming. It will also allow you to determine whether or not the style you are aspiring to is practical for your facial hair.

6) During early stages of growth, eyebrow pencils may be used to conceal uneven patches and to

define irregular borders. Select a shade that approximates your natural beard colour. You can also try a product called Clubman Color Comb Haircolor Touch Up, which is cream-based, quick drying, and shampoos out.

7) Have patience, and set a time limit prior to which you will not shave. This will prevent you from giving up prematurely.

8) Itching present during the first few weeks should subside once your skin adjusts to its new condition and whiskers soften with length.

9) The first time you shape your new beard, you may prefer to have a barber or professional stylist execute the shaping and define the neckline. If you undertake this yourself, proceed with caution. Keep in mind the cheek area is typically most flattering left natural.

10) When shaping your beard, use a safety razor rather than an electric trimmer as this reduces the risk of over-trimming and mistakes.

Selecting a Beard

1) Face size and shape are key factors when selecting a beard or moustache style. Consider how various styles will enhance or magnify individual features and overall appearance. Keep in mind that your beard may be of a different shade than your head hair, and may not grow in fully.

2) Social and professional limitations should also be considered, particularly during the initial phase of growth, as a developing beard lends a somewhat unkempt quality to your appearance.

3) Tips for selecting a beard type have remained fairly constant over the 20th century. Here is what Mrs C.E. Humphry wrote in her 1904, in her book, *Etiquette for Every Day*: "Men with long faces should have round beards, if any. But if a man's face is abnormally round and fat, he should wear an 'imperial,' as the narrow, long variety of Van Dyck beard is called. Oddly enough, it is the Americans who chiefly favour this form, though their faces, being long and narrow, need it less than any other."

4) For men with narrow, oblong, or irregular faces, a beard may soften features and create an oval

appearance. A beard which is full at the sides and shorter at the chin works well.

5) Narrow faces are best suited to beards that add fullness and create an oval perimeter. Rounded beards can conceal pointed or angular chins and jaw lines.

6) Round faces are flattered by narrow beards that accentuate vertical planes, drawing the eye down the length of the face. Moustaches divert attention inward from the circumference of the face. For a round face, squared-off sideburns, a short squared beard, or a triangular goatee draw attention to the vertical line of the face.

7) Short or bushy sideburns and thick beards emphasize fullness and should be avoided for round faces.

8) Square faces are softened by rounded beard and moustache styles. Sideburns create a box-like frame and should therefore be avoided. In general, moustaches draw attention to the centre of the face, away from prominent angles.

9) Oval faces suit nearly any style of facial hair. Choose a beard or moustache that enhances individual features. A prominent nose and ears are better suited to longer, fuller styles, whereas shorter styles enhance smaller features.

10) A small face looks best with a smaller moustache and beard shapes so as to avoid being overpowered.

11) Facial hair can balance a balding head and detract attention from a bare scalp.

12) A moustache can conceal thin lips and if upturned, can lighten up a down-turning mouth.

13) Long sideburns with a goatee tend to make thin faces appear more vertical. Pencil-thin lines tend to make thin or angular faces appear more so. A bushy moustache creates a horizontal line, which can make a thin face look fuller. A thin moustache achieves the opposite for a round face.

14) A goatee or chin curtain can disguise a pointy chin.

15) A full beard can effectively conceal a weak or double chin.

16) A soul patch can make a long face appear less drawn.

17) Short men are better suited to short, trimmed beard styles due to the persistent gnome associations.

Shaving preparations in the U.K., which includes aftershaves, razors and blades, realized sales of UK£ 274.8 million for the year ending January 2000.

GROWING A
BEARD OR MOUSTACHE

1) Do not shave at all for the first four to six weeks. Allowing your beard to progress naturally will prevent over-trimming and uneven shaping, and will give you a sense of whether the style you have selected is practical for your pattern of facial hair growth.

2) It is best to begin during a vacation or extended weekend, as you will be less self-conscious regarding your appearance and the remarks of others upon your fledgling whiskers.

3) The first two or three shaves should be performed cautiously if beard density is minimal. Once its growth is more profuse and greater length is achieved, you will be able to trim more freely.

4) Once your beard is suitably long, have a barber or stylist shape the boundaries and neckline.

5) If you are confident in your abilities to undertake this task yourself, use pictures of yourself as a reference and plot the boundaries of your beard with an eyebrow pencil. Keep your photographs on hand during the first few shaves to ensure your trimming is accurate.

6) Use short strokes, keeping the surrounding skin taut.

7) Trim away from the penciled boundary, taking care not to trim deeper than the established boundary. Uneven or rough areas can be refined once the initial shaping is complete.

8) It is generally best to leave the cheek area natural, using tweezers to pluck hairs that stray above the boundary of growth.

9) Itching is normal during the first several weeks. Wash and condition your beard as it grows to minimize itching and skin irritation, and to ensure your facial hair remains suitably clean. Conditioning will slightly soften coarser early growth.

Hair colour preference varies by region, with women in the northeast and north central areas of the U.S. favouring brown, and those in the southern and western states favouring black.

WASHING A BEARD

1) Your beard should be washed regularly, as frequently as you wash your hair. The same products used on your scalp hair may be used to wash and condition your beard, although these

should be of a mild formula to reduce the risk of irritation and excessive drying. Products designed specifically for facial hair are available.

2) If beard dandruff is a problem, regular dandruff shampoo, slightly diluted, may help.

3) Using a sparing amount of shampoo, massage your beard, working up a generous lather. Massaging your skin will loosen debris, skin flakes, and oils, and tone your skin.

4) Rinse thoroughly, ensuring all soap residue has washed away. Inadequate rinsing will promote itching, flaking, and matting. If desired, apply conditioner and rinse well. Conditioner will not produce a marked change in facial hair texture, but may subtly enhance softness and shine.

5) Pat your beard dry with a towel. Blow-drying will irritate skin and dry the hair shaft, and should therefore be avoided.

6) Once completely dry, comb your beard in the direction of growth using a wide-toothed comb. Gently work out tangles, then follow with a more vigorous brushing using a good quality hairbrush with sparse, firm bristles. Wet hair will stretch and pull, and it is not advisable to comb a damp beard.

Beard hair grows at 0.4 mm every 24 hours, so most men can have a new style in 7-21 days.

DYEING A BEARD

1) If your beard colour is uneven, highly variant to that of your scalp hair, prematurely or undesirably grey, you may wish to dye it using a temporary, semi-permanent, or permanent product.

2) It is inadvisable to use products intended for scalp hair, as these contain harsh chemicals which may irritate your skin, produce unsatisfactory results on facial hair, dry your beard hair, and are potential toxins.

3) Prior to undertaking a more permanent method, you may want to experiment with temporary dyes to determine a suitable colour. Start with a shade lighter than desired, as the final results may be darker than expected.

4) Before applying the dye, wash your beard to remove oily residues, but avoid vigorous scrubbing, as this will open pores and increase the risk of skin irritation.

5) Follow the manufacturer's instructions, as each product is different and will produce different results under different conditions. Performing a preliminary patch test will help you determine how a particular dye will alter your facial hair. Systematic application, working down from the uppermost region of beard growth to your chin, will ensure even coverage and prevent uneven, splotchy colour.

6) Most home dyeing kits (e.g., Just For Men) provide an applicator brush and are simple to use. The dye is brushed on, left in for five minutes, then rinsed away.

7) Head and facial hair dyes should never be applied to the eyebrows or eyelashes. To do so may cause blindness.

How to Use Moustache Wax

1) Take a smidgen of wax and rub it between your thumb and index finger.

2) Use sparingly and apply to dry hair with one finger.

3) Cover the entire moustache for an overall tidy look, or twirl points repeatedly between your thumb and forefingers. To achieve up-turning points, twirl with a technique much the same as snapping your fingers.

4) Keep in mind that most products will slightly darken the colour of your facial hair.

5) Reapply as required to maintain your style. Many products linger for more than a single face-washing, while the quantity of wax required to maintain a more extreme style or control a bushier moustache may be greater.

How to Apply False Facial Hair

Moustaches
1) Trim away any excess netting from the backing of the moustache. Take care not to sever the piece or trim too close to the hairline.

2) Hold the moustache against your lip and trace its outline with a light eyebrow pencil, then apply a

Be
No
Longer
Lather's slave
Treat yourself to
Burma-Shave

– Burma-Shave slogan,
c. 1930

light, even coat of spirit gum to this area of skin. Spirit gum is easily removed with rubbing alcohol and cotton swabs.

3) Centre the moustache above your lip, then gently press it on with your fingers, leaving approximately 1/8 inch between the base of the moustache and the rim of your upper lip. Applying direct, even pressure along its length will ensure it adheres and does not spring free.

4) It may be necessary to trim the moustache once affixed. Only trim away a slight amount at a time to prevent over-trimming.

Goatees

1) As with moustaches, trim the backing carefully.

2) Goatees should be centred on your chin, beginning about 1/2 inch beneath your lower lip, with a point extending to each corner of your mouth.

3) Trace its outline and apply spirit gum, then apply as with moustaches, using gentle pressure to ensure it stays on securely. Trim as required.

Full Beards and Sideburns

1) Trim, trace, and affix as with moustaches or goatees.

2) When applying a false beard, ensure its upper points are covered by or blended into your natural sideburns or hairline.

3) Sideburns should blend into your natural hair. Take care that each piece is centred evenly, and the ends reach an equal length.

You'll love your wife
You'll love her paw
You'll even love
Your mother-in-law
If you use
Burma-Shave

– Burma-Shave slogan,
c. 1932

Perfect Clipping & Trimming of Beards

Scissors Method

1) The best way to achieve accurate trimming is to invest in a pair of barber's shears. These narrow, long scissors will enable you to trim hard-to-reach or delicate areas. In addition, you should acquire a pair of short, blunt scissors for clipping around the ears and nostrils.

2) Use a long, thin, narrow comb to draw up the hair you wish to trim away. This measure will prevent over-trimming and cutting too deeply.

The comb will also facilitate even trimming as you progress from one area of your beard to another.

3) An electric beard trimmer is ideal for all-over shaping, shortening, and trimming broader, smoother areas of facial hair.

4) Before you begin trimming, ensure your beard is dry. Hair appears longer when wet, then springs shorter once dry.

5) Begin trimming by using the comb to isolate the length to be trimmed away. Work your way down the length of one side of your face, from ear to chin, then the other, taking care to trim each side evenly.

6) Beard grooming products condition, add shine, and can help maintain the shape of longer beards or more defined styles. Light hair grooming products may also be used; however, make sure they are natural hold, non-greasy, and are applied sparingly to avoid flaking, matting, or irritation.

Electric Shaver Method

1) A beard trimmer can be used on specific areas or passed over the body of your beard to achieve a uniform length.

2) Set the trim guard/comb to the desired length, keeping in mind it is easier to trim more away if your beard remains undesirably long than it is to reverse an excessively short trimming.

3) Comb your beard in the direction of growth, working out tangles and combing longer or stray hairs outward for even trimming.

4) When shaving, work your way evenly through your beard as with the comb and scissors method.

5) Begin with the upper boundary above your jaw, shaping the edge from your chin to your ears. Trim away from the hairline to avoid cutting too deeply into the body of your beard. Next, trim the underside of your jaw, from the centre of your chin to below each earlobe.

6) Select the comb attachment corresponding with your desired beard length and pass the shaver over the body of your beard, trimming and tapering its length and defining the edges and sideburns. A more uniform shave can be achieved by starting at the sideburn area and trimming downward to your chin.

Lawyers, doctors
Sheiks and bakers
Mountaineers and
undertakers
Make their bristly beards
behave
By using brushless
Burma-Shave

— Burma-Shave slogan,
c. 1932

Scissors Method

1) Prepare by moistening the hair then combing it straight downward over your lips. Do not force the hair to lie flat, as it will return to its natural direction of growth once dry, and you may discover you have trimmed it too short.

2) Using narrow, pointed scissors, trim outward from the centre of your lip to each corner, using a comb to gauge how much to trim away. Holding the scissors at a diagonal will give you greater control and ensure the line trimmed is straight.

3) To give your moustache a straight lower edge, or to attain a pencil-thin style, the easiest method is to use a comb and electric trimmer or barber shears.

4) Once you have achieved the desired shape, use scissors to clip away stray, excessively long, or unkempt hairs from the body of the moustache.

5) Pomade, beeswax, or moustache wax can be used to give shape to longer moustaches. Apply sparingly and work through the whiskers with your fingertips. These products tend to add shine, and will darken the shade of your moustache.

Electric Shaving Method

1) Prepare your moustache for trimming as with the comb and scissors method, but ensuring hair is dry.

2) Trim away from the moustache hairline; define the upper edge below the nostrils.

3) If worn with a beard, using a comb attachment to blend the outer edges into the beard growth, trim from the centre of your mouth to the corners.

4) If your face is otherwise clean-shaven, taper the moustache as desired, using a comb attachment and working your way from the centre to the corners of your mouth. You may also want to blend the moustache downwards from its upper edge of growth to the rim of your upper lip, reducing the density of growth through its mid-portion.

5) Define the lower edge using a comb and the electric shaver, taking care to trim gradually to avoid cutting too short.

A 19th-century beard dye recipe: To dye the hair, beard, or whiskers, take the oil of costus and myrtle, of each an ounce; mix them in a leaden mortar, add liquid pitch, juice of walnut leaves, and laudanum, of each half an ounce, gall nuts, black lead, and frankincense, of each a drachma; and a sufficient quantity of mucilage of gum arabic, infused in a concoction of nut galls. The head, whiskers, and beard, after being shaved, are to be rubbed three times a day.

STEPS TO THE
PERFECT DRY SHAVE

1) If your beard is relatively coarse, you will not attain as close a shave using a beard trimmer or electric razor as with a safety razor and lather. Those with sensitive skin may find that performing an initial shave with an electric razor, then following with a wet razor and cream or foam may reduce irritation and ingrown hairs.

2) Wash and dry your face to remove oil and residue that might otherwise clog the shaver. Ensure your whiskers are completely dry, as damp hair is more difficult to trim with an electric shaver and is prone to snaring and pulling.

3) Spritz the shaver screen with an aerosol lubricant before beginning your shave.

4) Shave against the lie of the hair, using gentlr pressure. Use your free hand to identify missed patches.

5) Electric shavers tend to generate heat the longer they operate. Beginning your shave with the more tender areas will reduce irritation to sensitive skin.

6) Use a stiff brush to sweep whiskers from razor heads, or beneath foil screens, otherwise clogging may result and the closeness of the shave achieved will be reduced.

7) Replace the shaver's heads regularly, as per the manufacturer's recommendation.

STEPS TO THE
PERFECT WET SHAVE

1) Consider shaving during or immediately following a hot shower, as the water and steam will soften the hair shaft. Look for a steam-proof shaving mirror that can be hung in the shower.

2) Avoid shaving right before or after strenuous exercise, as perspiration may cause skin irritation. Sunscreen, salt water, and exposure to strong sunlight (i.e., during the summer) immediately after shaving can also dry and irritate the skin.

3) Menthol-containing products may close the pores and stiffen your beard, making shaving more difficult and irritation more probable.

I will drop in his way some obscure epistles of love; wherein by the colour of his beard, the shape of his leg, the manner of his gait, the expressure of his eye, forehead, and complexion, he shall find himself most feelingly personated.

– William Shakespeare, *Twelfth Night*

4) Use a clean, sharp blade as this will require less pressure to cut through the hairs, and will reduce the risk of nicks, cuts, and general skin abrasion.

5) Wash your face to open the pores and remove oily residues. Warm water will soften your beard, enabling the razor to make a cleaner cut with less friction and therefore less irritation.

6) Apply cream, foam, gel, or soap, building a generous lather with your fingertips or a good-quality shaving brush. This will keep your beard wet and reduce the friction between the blade and your skin. Cream products will reduce irritation to sensitive skin. Normal to oily skin is better suited to gels and foams, although these products may dry and coarsen the beard, making it more difficult to shave. In prolonged contact with regular soap, the skin tends to dry and, as such, soap is a practical but less than ideal shaving aid.

7) Begin with the smoother facial regions, as this hair requires less time to soften, while coarser, denser areas of growth will require a longer soak.

8) Shave in the direction of hair growth, with attention to areas that switch direction (under the chin, the length of the throat). This will prevent ingrown hairs and minimize irritation.

9) For a close shave, make a second pass against the lie of the hair once the initial shave is complete.

10) Long, smooth strokes are less irritating to the skin and ultimately produce a closer shave.

11) Rinse the razor blade often to prevent clogging, which can result in nicks and cuts.

12) Finish by splashing cold water on your face to rinse away shaving residue and to close your pores. This will stem bleeding from small cuts, and tone the skin.

13) A moist alum stick may be used to disinfect and cauterize persistently bleeding nicks or cuts.

14) A good quality, light moisturizer may be applied immediately after shaving to restore the natural moisture balance and to soothe the skin. A similar effect can be achieved with aftershave, although it may irritate sensitive skin or deeper nicks and cuts.

15) Apply an alcohol-free aftershave to soothe the skin and restore its moisture. Alcohol is extremely drying and promotes ingrown hairs, thus all shaving products that contain it should be avoided.

Courtesy of Darryl DeLozier.

16) Persistent razor bumps often respond well to exfoliating scrubs, or using mild glycerine soap and a soft face cloth. Scrub gently, moving over the affected area using a circular motion.

17) Witch hazel applied with cotton swabs will astringe and disinfect ingrown hairs, cuts, and other sites of acute skin irritation. Similarly, tea tree oil may be applied to facial blemishes and ingrown hairs to reduce inflammation and draw out infection.

USING A SHAVING BRUSH

1) The best results are achieved with a natural badger bristle brush (though these are often expensive) and a proper shaving mug.

2) Use a glycerin-based shaving soap or cream, which will lather well with water.

3) Wet your brush with hot water and brush the soap in your mug with a vigourous stirring motion. Continue until a solid, consistent lather forms. Some argue it is best to use a slightly watery lather first to moisten the skin, soften hair, and to prevent drying out, then moving to a thicker lather.

4) Apply lather under the chin first and then in small circles, moving upward over the rest of the face.

5) When you reach your upper lip, splay the brush with your middle finger (so as to avoid nasal intrusions!).

6) If your beard is dense, massage the lather with your fingers then reapply with the brush.

7) Reapply lather as often as necessary throughout the shave.

8) When finished, rinse your brush with warm water and hang to dry with the bristles pointing downward.

Wet facial hair is 70 percent easier to remove than dry.

SHAVING WITH AN OPEN RAZOR

1) Shaving Hand: the razor should be held in your right or left hand, as appropriate to your handedness. The blade is held facing downward, with your thumb on the underside and forefinger on the top at the blade-handle joint. The handle

Proper Use of Chemical Depilatories:

Moisten beard area with warm water, lather with mild soap and rinse.

Apply depilatory paste made from powder or cream to half of the beard area and let set for 2 to 3 minutes (barfum sulfide) or 10 minutes (calcium thioglycolate).

Remove depilatory with moistened wooden tongue depressor, scraping in the direction of hair growth.

Rapidly rinse face three times, using soap between rinses, to prevent facial irritation.

Follow the same procedure on the other half of the beard area. A cool washcloth may be held against the face for 3 to 5 minutes to reduce irritation.

Apply topical corticosteroids, cocoa butter or emollient if pruritus is present.

Use above regimen every 3 to 5 days.

— *AFP*, September 1988

angles upward across the remaining fingers and is anchored between your ring and pinkie fingers, while the blade extends outward past your thumb.

2) Tensioning Hand: Your free hand remains dry and is used to stretch taut the skin below the razor.

3) When shaving, each stroke should be gentle, long, and sustained. Short, brisk strokes will abrade the skin and increase the risk of cutting and nicking.

4) Begin the shave on the side corresponding with your handedness (right for right-handed, left for left-handed).

5) To mark the base of each sideburn, draw a finger-line through the shaving foam, ensuring the length is even. The first stroke should be made from the base of the sideburn to the jaw. Following the direction of beard growth, stretch the skin taut and draw the blade down the cheek in a smooth stroke extending along the neck. Work your way inward in long strokes, wiping the blade clean after each pass.

6) Once you have reached the centre of the face, proceed to the opposite side and shave as above, leaving the nose and chin region for last.

7) Shave from the centre of the chin outward, then under the jaw. Shave upward from the point of the chin to the base of the lower lip.

8) Drawing the blade downward, shave beneath the nostrils and along the upper lip.

9) For a closer shave, pass the razor against the direction of growth, beginning with the smooth regions of the face but reversing the strokes detailed above.

10) Hot towels, facial massage, or after shave products (talcum powder, moisturizer, lotion) may be applied to finish the shave.

HOW TO HONE A RAZOR

1) Hones are typically rectangular blocks of abrasive synthetic or natural material, and are used for sharpening open razors. Generally, synthetic surfaces are used to produce a sharp edge, while natural hones are well suited for producing fine, long-lasting razor edges.

2) Following the manufacturer's recommendations, lubricate the hone surface with water, oil, or lather.

3) Holding the razor with one hand and the hone block with the other, position the razor flat against the hone, in the upper right corner, edge facing inward.

4) Slide the blade diagonally and down across the hone, applying gentle pressure. Pass the blade from its heel to toe along the hone with the downward stroke.

5) Rotate the blade so the opposite edge is against the hone and pass it as above, from upper left to lower right corners of the hone.

6) Next, perform a reverse stroke, passing the blade along the hone from lower left to upper right, and lower right to upper left corners. The blade should be positioned as above; however, no pressure should be applied as the blade is pushed upward.

7) After each pair of strokes, test the blade to ensure sharpness is adequate, but over-sharpening is avoided.

Ben Lassen, Library of Congress, LC-USZC2 1010.

How to Strop a Razor

1) A variety of styles of strop are available. Barbers typically prefer hanging strops, which consist of a canvas side for cleaning the razor's edge and a leather side for achieving a smooth finish, or whetted edge.

2) Position the razor near the top of the strop with the cutting edge facing upward.

3) Apply light pressure as you draw the razor across the strop, passing the blade diagonally from heel to toe.

4) Rotate the blade so the cutting edge is pointing downward then draw the blade upward to the top of the strop in a similar stroke. Do not apply pressure during this motion.

5) Rotate the blade and continue to pass it up and down the length of the strop until a desired sharpness is achieved.

Ho, pretty page, with
the dimpled chin
That never has known
the barber's shear
All your wish is woman
to win
That's the way that boys
begin,
Wait till you come to
Forty Year

— William Thackeray,
The Age of Wisdom

HOW TO GET
RID OF A BEARD

1) To enhance the ritual, consider having your barber perform the task for you with hot towels and a straight razor.

2) If you have an electric razor, trim away as much dry hair as you can first.

3) Shaving during or immediately following a hot shower can reduce skin irritation and make the shaving process a smoother one.

4) Your skin may be more sensitive following a shaving vacation. Use mild shaving products and a clean, sharp blade to reduce nicks, cuts, and skin abrasions.

5) Scrub your face gently with warm water to soften your beard, then apply a thick lather of foam using your fingertips or a good-quality shaving brush.

6) Begin with the smoother facial regions, progressing to areas of coarser, denser growth, which may require a longer soak before they are supple enough to shave.

7) For a close shave, make a second pass against the lie of the hair once the initial shave is complete.

8) Be prepared for a shock if you've not seen your bare face for a while. Plan your next move.

FACIAL HAIR RECIPES

BEARDS

Poet's Beard

1) Shave the cheeks, upper lip, throat, and immediately below the lower lip.

2) Leave intact the hair at the point of the chin, and extending a short length along the jaw line.

3) Using a razor, form a defined edge that blends along the jaw line into the thicker chin hair.

4) Trim the beard into a short, blunt-pointed beard.

Chin Curtain Beard

1) Shave the cheeks clean in a slope following the sideburn line, downward to a point two inches above the jaw.
2) Form a curving upper beard edge that extends from the sideburn line to the chin, leaving chin whiskers intact.
3) Shave away the moustache and hair beneath the lower lip.
4) Groom the beard length and chin whiskers to a dull point, using scissors and a comb.

Franz Josef Beard

1) Shave the cheeks in a slope extending from the sideburns to the outer tips of the moustache.
2) Shave the chin and lower lip, forming a sharp line of whiskers that arcs over the upper lip.
3) Shave the throat, forming a curved edge along the jaw.

Circle Beard

1) Shave all hair from the cheeks and throat.
2) Leave a rounded beard that extends from the moustache to the chin.
3) Trim the uppermost moustache edge into a curve that blends into the outer beard boundary.
4) Groom the moustache and beard hairs to the desired length using scissors or an electric trimmer.
5) Clip the lower edge of the moustache flush with the upper lip.

Roman T Beard

1) Following the goatee and moustache style, shave the beard clean, leaving only the chin whiskers.
2) Trim the beard to a long point, grooming with wax to hold its shape.
3) The moustache should be allowed to grow to a length great enough to wax into extended horizontal points.

Cathedral Beard

1) This style requires several months of growth to achieve.
2) Trim the cheek area to a smooth length, shorter than the chin and moustache whiskers.
3) Allow the moustache and chin whiskers to grow freely, grooming them downward into a broad curtain that extends beyond the collar.

Spade Beard

1) Allow the beard and moustache to grow freely for several months.
2) The cheek line is left natural, as is the moustache.
3) Using scissors, shape the chin and jaw whiskers to a broad, blunt point that curves from the ears to the neck.

Stiletto Beard

1) The beard and moustache are allowed to grow naturally.
2) Wax the outer moustache length to extended points, curving slightly outwards.
3) Using scissors, trim the lower beard whiskers to a point extending a few inches below the chin.
4) The cheek line may be left natural or shaved in a sharp edge extending downward to the moustache.

Amish-style (Dutch) Beard

1) Although this style requires at least three months' natural growth, one can achieve a shorter version if desired.
2) Shave all hair from the cheeks to the base of the smile lines, forming a curving line from the sideburns to the chin.
3) With scissors and a comb, trim the beard from the sideburns to the bottom of the smile lines, working down each side of the face to achieve a uniform length.
4) Using a safety razor, shave away the moustache and define the growth line of the beard.

Soul Patch

1) Shave all hair from the cheeks, throat, and chin.
2) Shave the upper lip clean.
3) Only the hair immediately beneath the lower lip should remain.
4) These whiskers can be shaped into a triangular patch, with angles reaching a point in the centre of the chin; create a solid square, shaving straight down from the lower lip to the chin; or form a softer circular tuft.

Shaft-style goatee

1) Trim the entire beard to a uniform length of about 1/4 inch. This is best achieved using an electric trimmer, selecting the 1.5 setting.
2) Shave the cheeks clean, leaving a curving hairline from the sideburns to the outer tips of the moustache.
3) Similarly, shave under the jaw, forming a curving line stretching from each ear to the point at which the throat and lower jaw meet, just above the Adam's apple.
4) Trim the uppermost moustache edge, beneath the nose, defining a horizontal line.
5) Leaving the natural hairline intact, trim above the upper lip.
6) Shape the whiskers between the lower lip and chin to form a narrow stripe, or soul patch.

Goatee with Moustache

1) The cheeks and throat are clean-shaven.
2) Shave the chin whiskers, leaving hair only on the region below the boundary of the mouth. This hair may be trimmed short or groomed to a longer point.
3) Shave below the lower lip, removing the "soul patch" whiskers.
4) Shave the area between the corners of the mouth and the chin, forming a sharp boundary where the chin whiskers begin.
5) Trim the moustache to the desired style and length.

MOUSTACHES

Military Moustache

1) Shave all facial hair, leaving the moustache intact.
2) Using a razor, trim away moustache whiskers that extend beyond the corners of the mouth.
3) With scissors and a thin, narrow comb, create a sharp lower edge, trimming the whiskers along the uppermost ridge of the lip.

Fu Manchu Moustache

1) Shave the cheeks and chin clean, leaving a moustache that curves from the upper lip to a point lateral to the bottom edge of the lower lip.
2) Trim the inner area of the upper lip whiskers flush with the uppermost edge of the lip.
3) Using a razor, shave the outer edges of the moustache into a downward curve, following the natural slope of the mouth.
4) The outer whiskers require growth, drooping beyond the chin.
5) Moustache wax may be applied to the longer whiskers or they may be left natural.

Handlebar Moustache

1) This style is similar to the Fu Manchu; however, its lines are thicker and growth more dense.
2) Following the line of the upper lip, shave the moustache into a downward slope, leaving a finger width of hair.
3) The outer regions of the moustache require a thick length in order to fill in, forming longer, denser tendrils than worn in the Fu Manchu.

Clark Gable-style Moustache

1) The face should be clean-shaven, leaving only the moustache whiskers intact.
2) Using an electric shaver, trim the moustache hair to a length of approximately 1/4 inch.
3) Trim away any moustache whiskers that progress beyond the corners of the mouth.
4) Beginning in the centre, beneath the nose, trim each side in a diagonal line that passes sharply from the nose to the corner of the mouth.
5) Use a safety razor to shave clean the vertical crease running from the base of the nose to the upper lip.
6) Trim the lower moustache edge, forming a clean, straight line.

Chaplin Moustache

1) The cheeks and chin are clean-shaven.
2) With a razor, shave away the upper moustache, leaving only a finger width of growth on each side of the midpoint of the upper lip.
3) Trim the whiskers sharply along the upper lip edge.
4) Trim between the nostrils and the upper moustache edge to form a clean line.

Dali Moustache
1) Shave all facial hair, leaving the upper moustache whiskers intact to a point extending slightly beyond the outer edge of the lips.
2) The centre-most area of the moustache should be trimmed relatively short, using scissors.
3) Allow the whiskers to grow longer in length, gradually increasing toward the corners of the mouth.
4) The outermost whiskers are worn long enough to wax into vertical extensions. Apply wax sparingly, working it into the hair and sculpting long points upward from each corner of the mouth.

SIDEBURNS

Sideburns: Standard Issue
1) The face is clean-shaven, with only broad patches extending from the hairline to a point between the earlobe and point of jaw articulation.
2) Use an electric trimmer to groom the sideburns to a desired length.
3) With a razor, create a sharp, horizontal lower edge.

Mutton Chops
1) Shave the throat, lips, and chin.
2) Leave all cheek hair intact from the hairline to the point beneath the outer edge of the eyes.
3) Shave two fingers width along the jaw, creating a sloping lower edge that follows two inches above the natural jaw line.
4) Use an electric trimmer to achieve the desired length in the body of the whiskers.
5) The upper edge is left natural.

Fun 'n Folly Costumes & Novelties
tel: 1-888-267-9271
costumefun.com

United Mask & Party Manufacturing, Inc.
8081 Commercial Blvd.
Sebring, FL 33876
tel: 863-655-MASK (6275)
fax: 863-655-4350
unitedmaskandparty.com

International Magic & Fun Shop
tel: 281-332-8142
fax: 281-554-6618
fun-shop.com

Broadway Costumes™, Inc
1100 West Cermak Rd., Second Floor
Chicago, IL 60608
tel: 312-829-6400
toll free: 1-800-397-3316
fax: 312-829-8621
broadwaycostumes.com

Malabar Limited
14 McCaul St.
Toronto, ON M5T 1V6
tel: (416) 598-2581
fax: (416) 598-3296
malabar.net

BIBLIOGRAPHY

Books

Adams Jr., Russell B., and King, C. *Gillette: The Man and His Wonderful Shaving Device*. Toronto: Little, Brown and Co., 1978.

The Art and Science of Shaving. Milford, CT: Warner-Lambert Co., 1994.

Alyson Almanac. Boston: Alyson Publications, 1990.

Andrews, William. *At the Sign of the Barber Pole: Studies in Hirsute History*. Detroit: Singing Tree Press, 1969.

Asser, Joyce. *Historic Hairdressing*. London: Sir Isaac Pitman and Sons, 1966.

Banner, Lois W. *American Beauty*. New York: Alfred A. Knopf, 1983.

Beers, Mark H., *et al. Merck Manual*. 7th Ed. Whitehorse, YT: Merck Research Laboratories, 1999.

Berg, Charles. *The Unconscious Significance of Hair*. Washington: Guild Press, 1951.

Boston, Lloyd. *Men of Color: Fashion, History, Fundamentals*. New York: Artisan, 1998.

Bunkin, Helen. *Beards, Beards, Beards*. Montgomery, AL: Green Street Press, 2000.

Charles, Ann and De Anfrasio, Roger. *The History of Hair*. New York: Bonanza Books, 1970.

Chevannes, Barry. *Rastafari: Roots and Ideology*. Syracuse, NY: Syracuse University Press, 1994.

Cooper, Wendy. *Hair: Sex, Society, Symbolism*. New York: Stein & Day, 1971.

Corson, Richard. *Fashions in Hair: The First Five Thousand Years*. London: Peter Owen, 1965.

de Zemler, Charles. *Once Over Lightly: The Story of Man and His Hair*. New York: self-published, 1939.

Dunkling, Leslie and Foley, John. *The Guinness Book of Beards and Moustaches*. Middlesex: Guinness Publishing Ltd., 1990.

Erardi, Glenn and Peck, Pauline C. *Mustache Cups, Timeless Victorian Treasures*. Atglen, PA: Schiffer Books, 1999.

Grief, Martin. *The Gay Book of Days*. New York: Main Street Press, 1989.

Grosswirth, Marvin. *The Art of Growing a Beard*. New York: Jarrow Press, Inc., 1971.

Horn, Barbara Lee. *The Age of Hair: Evolution and Impact of Broadway's First Rock Musical*. Westport, CT: Greenwood Press, 1991.

Jones, Dylan. *Haircults: Fifty Years of Styles and Cuts*. London: Thames & Hudson, 1990.

McNeill, Daniel. *The Face: A Guided Tour*. London: Hamish Hamilton, 1998.

Panati, Charles. *Panati's Extraordinary Origins of Everyday Things*. New York: Perennial Library, 1987.

Perret, Jean Jacques. *La Pogonotomia*. Milano, Italy: il Polifilo, n.d.

Pinfold, Wallace G. *A Closer Shave: Man's Daily Search for Perfection*. New York: Artisan, 1999.

Polhemus, Ted. *Street Style: From Sidewalk to Catwalk*. London: Thames and Hudson, 1995.

The Razor Anthology. A collection of selected articles about razors, reprinted from monthly issues of Knife World. Knoxville, TN: Knife World Publications, 1995.

Reynolds, Reginald. *Beards: Their Social Standing, Religious Involvements, Decorative Possibilities, and Value in Offence and Defence Through the Ages*. Garden City, NY: Doubleday & Co., 1949.

Ritchie, Roy and Stewart, Ron. *The Standard Guide to Razors*. Paducah, KY: Collector Books, 1995.

Rosetree, Rose. *The Power of Face Reading*. Sterling: WIW Press, 1989.

Severn, Bill. *The Long and the Short of It: Five Thousand Years of Fun and Fury over Hair*. New York: David McKay Co., 1971.

Spillane, Mary. *Presenting Yourself: A Personal Image Guide for Men*. London: Judy Piatkus Ltd., 1994.

Wilcox, R. Turner. *Dictionary of Costumes*. New York: Charles Scribner's Sons, 1969.

Woodforde, John. *The History of Vanity*. London: Routledge and K. Paul, 1971.

Wright, Les, ed. *The Bear Book: Readings in the History and Evolution of a Gay Male Subculture*. New York: Harrington Park Press, 1997.

_____. *The Bear Book II*. New York: Harrington Park Press, 2001.

Ziff, Larzer. *Puritanism in America: New Culture in a New World*. New York: Viking, 1973.

Articles

Adamick, Paula. "Face—the final frontier." *Globe & Mail* (December 9, 2000): R3.

Addison, William E. "Beardedness as a factor in perceived masculinity." *Perceptual Motor Skills* 68:3 (June, 1989): 921-2.

Az-Zuhri, Br. Bilal. "The Islamic Ruling on Shaving the Beard." *Nida-ul Islam* 22 (February-March, 1998).

"Blame it all on the beards." *The Economist* 316:7664 (July 21, 1990): 49.

Brock-Utne, J.G., Brodsky, J.B., and Haddow, G.R. "Bearded Sikhs and tracheal intubation." *Anesthesia & Analgesia* 91:2 (August, 2000): 494.

"Sexual activity and beard growth." *Nature* 226:252 (June 27, 1970): 1277-8.

Brookhiser, Richard. "By the hair of your chinny chin chin." *Forbes* 158:12 (November 18, 1996): S132.

Campbell, Duncan. "Whisker riskers dodge stubble trouble." *Guardian* (March 31, 2000).

Carroll, Timothy J. "Don't get too familiar with my face." *Wall Street Journal* (December 11, 1984): 22.

"China Warns of Beards' Harm." *Wall Street Journal* (May 18, 1994): A10.

Curran, John and Pollard, Brian. "Beards, academia, and anaesthesia: a controlled study." *British Medical Journal* 313:7072 (December 21, 1996): 1643.

Deitch, Joseph. "Rembrandt would have loved him! New York Times newsroom receptionist sports a 26-inch mustache." *Editor and Publisher* 119 (August 2, 1986): 13.

"Disney shaves facial hair ban." *Workforce* 79:5 (May, 2000): 26.

Drakes, Shellene. "Boxer fights for beard." *Toronto Star* (December 3, 1999).

Dunn, J. F. Jr. "Pseudofolliculitis barbae." *American Family Physician* 38:3 (September, 1988): 169-74.

Duffy, Bryce. "The Cutting Edge." *Shift* (April, 1998): 65-70.

Edwards, Owen. " Lip service." *GQ* 64:7 (July, 1994): 33.

"Effects of sexual activity on beard growth in man." *Nature* 226:248 (May 30, 1970): 869-70.

Faibes, Daniela. "Bearded Girls." *Omni* 6 (September 1984): 40.

Gorman, James. "Wash that mustache!" *New York Times* 146:252 (September 9, 1997): C4.

Field, L. M. "Sideburn hairline reconstruction by flap techniques." *Journal of Dermatological Surgery* 21:9 (September, 1995): 771-5.

Gottlieb, Bill. "Posin'." *DownBeat* 56:9 (September, 1989): 33.

Graham, David. "Pumped up with pride." *Toronto Star* (June 23, 2001): M1.

Green, Penelope. "Stubble trouble." *Men's Fashions of the Times* 70, n.d.

Gup, Ted. "If a mustache becomes you, don't cut it off." *Smithsonian* 28:9 (December, 1997): 160.

"Hair to the chief." *Time* 151:1 (January 12, 1998): 24.

Hamilton, D. R. and Kobylik, B. "Infection risk in the bearded patient." *Infection Control and Hospital Epidemiology* 9:22 (February, 1988): 55.

Heinzl, John. "Young men driven by blond ambition." *Globe & Mail* (November 3, 2000): M1.

Hou, T.S., Davis, M.D., el-Azhary, R., Corbett, J. F., and Gibson, L.E. "Beard dermatitis due to para-phenylenediamine use in Arabic men." *Journal of the American Academy of Dermatology* 44:5 (May, 2001): 867-9.

Howard, Manny. "The thin black line." *GQ* 69:6 (June, 1999): 199.

Kaus, Mickey. "Facially correct." *The New Republic* 204:9 (March 4, 1991): 42.

Kreyche, Gerald F. "The mustache: man's last bastion of individuality." *USA Today* 118:2532 (September, 1989): 98.

Lacey, J. H. "Anorexia nervosa and a bearded female saint." *British Medical Journal* (Clin Res Ed) 285:6357 (December, 1982): 1816-7.

LaFerla, Ruth. "Beards are hair today." *Toronto Star* (March 10, 2001): M4.

MacPherson, A., Balint, J., and Basco, J. "Beard calcium concentration as a marker for coronary heart disease as affecting supplementation with micronutrients including selenium." *Analyst* 120:3 (March, 1995): 871-5.

Martin, David. "Saying bye-bye to a very special patch of thatch." *Globe & Mail* (July 23, 2001): A16.

McCain, Diana Ross. "Circuses, magic, and other entertainment." *Early American Life* 26:6 (December, 1995): 40.

Moller, Herbert. "The accelerated development of youth: beard growth as a biological marker." *Society for Comparative Study of Society and History* 29:4 (October, 1987): 748-762.

Moritz, Robert. "A Brief History of Whiskers, Starting with God." *GQ* (September, 2000): 345-350.

Nordstrom, R.E., Greco, M., and Vitagliano, T. "Correction of sideburn defects after facelift operations. " *Aesthetic Plastic Surgery* 24:6 (Nov-Dec, 2000): 429-32.

Nunez, M., Miralles, E.S., Arrazola, J.M., and Ledo, A. "Unilateral localized failure of beard growth." *Pediatric Dermatology* 13:2 (Mar-Apr, 1996): 143-5.

Ott, Michael. "Wilgefortis." *Catholic Encyclopedia*: 1913.

Parker, N. "The moustache: a scientific study." *Australia/New Zealand Journal of Psychiatry* 4:1 (March, 1970): 49-54.

Plewka, Karl. "Must 'ave a mustache." *Interview* 29:11 (November, 1999): 86.

Pope, Hugh. "Turkish mustaches, or the lack thereof, bristle with meaning." *Wall Street Journal* (May 15, 1997): A1.

Power, William. "For new chairman, hair apparent still applies." *Wall Street Journal* (September 15, 1994): C1

Recchi, Ray. "No facial hair allowed in 17 state police forces." *Knight-Ridder/Tribune News Services* (July 26, 1993): 0726k2522.

Scherer, Barrymore Laurence. "Read their lips." *New York Times Magazine* 140 (September 23, 1990): S52.

Shelby, Barry. "Debating beards." *World Press Review* 43:12 (December, 1996): 34.

Skretvedt, O.T. and Loschiavo, J.G. "Effect of facial hair on the face seal of negative pressure respirators." *American Independent Hygienists Association Journal* 45:1 (January, 1984): 63-6.

Snigurowicz, Diana. "Sex, simians, and spectacle in Nineteeth-century France; Or, how to tell a 'man' from a monkey." *Canadian Journal of Natural History* 34 (April, 1999): 51.

Snowden, Lynn. "Facial Attraction." *Cosmopolitan* 212:6 (June, 1992): 216-220.

Stoddard, Maynard Good. "To beard or not to beard." *Saturday Evening Post* 269:1 (jan-Feb, 1997): 46.

"The subtle art of stubble." Newsweek 106 (December 9, 1985): 62.

Terry, Roger L. and Krantz, John H. "Dimensions of trait attributions associated with eyeglasses, men's facial hair, and women's hair length." *Journal of Applied Social Psychology* 23:21 (November, 1993): 1757.

Vallis, C. P. "Hair transplantation to the upper lip to create a moustache. Case report." *Plastic Reconstructive Surgery* 54:5 (November, 1974): 606-8.

Varadarajan, Tunku. "Manly men keep stiff upper lip, and a bare one." *Wall Street Journal* (September 22, 2000): W17.

Wachter, Wally. "Mugs and straight razors fascinated little shavers." *Herald*, Sharon, PA (August 10, 1996).

Wark, John T. "Trends: Face it—that fuzzy stubble on men is really hip." *Detroit News* (October 5, 1995).

Videos

Paget, John. *Almost Elvis: Elvis Impersonators and Their Quest for the Crown*. VHS.

Websites

news.bbc.co.uk/hi/english/world/americas/newsid_465000/4652
    20.stm

members.aol.com/beardguy/beards.htm

www.ananova.com/news/story/sm_120779.html

www.muttaqun.com/beard.html

www.jb-photodesign.de/beardcategories.htm

www.lamorski.de/beard-2000.html

www.boinklabs.com/pipermail/beerlist/2000-
    February/000024.html

www.madsci.org/posts/archives/feb98/884562233.An.r.html

www.qss.org/articles/beard.html

members.tripod.co.uk/surfergal

www.newswire.ca/releases/December2000/21/c5927.html

youngbeards.freeservers.com

planet.ten.net/~nbc

www.beards.org

www.rocknroll.force9.co.uk/faceHair/Facehair.htm

www.costumefun.com/h/w/wigchr4.htm

www.folica.com/haircolor/color-comb_touchup.htm

www.shoplet.com/software/db/075528.html

www.garneaux.com/hair/wigs_hairpieces.htm

www.beardshampoo.com

store.yahoo.com/corradocutlery/pinprod.html

www.zorrapredictions.com/fshui/fs_face/face13.htm

beauty.about.com/style/beauty/cs/formenonlymenu/index.htm

www.totallyhk.com/LifeStyle/Shopping/Article/
FullText_asp_ArticleID-20010212113424704.asp

members.aol.com/antlavelle

www.euphoria.force9.co.uk/realhumour/beards/credits.html

www.rocknroll.force9.co.uk/faceHair/Facehair.htm

www.newswire.ca/releases/December2000/21/c5927.html

youngbeards.freeservers.com

www.geocities.com/FashionAvenue/5199/handlbar.htm

www.handlebarclub.org.uk

www.rocknroll.force9.co.uk/faceHair/Facehair.htm

www.newswire.ca/releases/December2000/21/c5927.html

geocities.com/sentell2001

www.utas.edu.au/docs/sideburn/sideburn.htm

www.happybunny.co.uk/html/sideburns.html

www.utas.edu.au/docs/sideburn/sideburn.htm

home.clara.net/chime/hotspankyculture/sideburns/
supertastic_sideburns_sideshow.htm

www.ukans.edu/~kansite/wwi-l/msg01077.html

pub40.ezboard.com/fhughjackmanfrm1.showMessage?topicID=3
9.topic

www.xnet2.com/bomp/searchable/9903/msg00920.html

www.the-light.com/beardnmoustache/wwwboard.html

www.forbes.com/global/2000/0403/0306023a_print.html

provide.net/~geraldo/yes_that.htm

ednet.edc.gov.ab.ca/k_12/curriculum/bySubject/cfs/cosmet/
cos-slg.pdf

ffgallery.tripod.com

www.moustache.de/linkse.htm

www.ma.adfa.oz.au/~mark/misc.dir/beards.html

sports.yahoo.com/nl/news/ap/990216/ap-reds-facial.html

www.ragadio.com/oafh

www.theage.com.au/entertainment/20000328/
A33496-2000Mar27.html

www.quickshave.com/egypt.htm

www.islam.org.au/articles/22/beard.htm

www.conair.com

www.MACH3.com

www.clinique.com/mentip.html

users.erols.com/tjflynn/Shaving_tips.html

www.artofshaving.com/shavingtips.html

www.insideedge.com

www.inetarena.com/~georgia/index.htm

www.delphi.com/n/main.asp?webtag=beardedwomen&nav=start

www.bluecalabash.com.au/goatee

www.goateestyle.com

www.goatee.org

members.aol.com/bearguy/color.htm

members.aol. com/beardguy/groom1.htm

www.ehow.com/eHow/eHow/0,1053,874,00.html

www.clinique.com/mentip.html

www.artofshaving.com/shavingtips.html

www.insideedge.com/edge_lookingyourbest.shtm

www.wahlclipper.com/html/html/styling-guide_beard.html

www.wahlclipper.com/html/html/styling-guide_beard.html

www.ehow.com/eHow/eHow/0, 1053, 874,00.html

www.clinique.com/mentip.html

www.artofshaving.com/shavingtips.html

www.insideedge.com/edge_lookingyourbest.shtm

users.erols.com/tjflynn/Shaving_tips.html

www.hair3x.com/men.htm

members.aol.com/beardguy/beard036.htm

www.wahl.com/html/html/styling-guide_beard.html

wahl.com/html/styling-guide_beard.html

www.artofshaving.com/shavingtips.html

www.jan.ucc.nau.edu/~jec/FacialHair.htm

www.jb-photodesign.de/beardcategories.htm

members.aol.com/beardguy/groom1.htm

ALLAN PETERKIN is a Toronto psychiatrist and journalist, and the author of *The Bald-Headed Hermit & The Artichoke: An Erotic Thesaurus* (Arsenal Pulp, 1999).